When Terrorism Hits Home

How Prepared Are State and Local Law Enforcement?

Lois M. Davis, K. Jack Riley, Greg Ridgeway,
Jennifer Pace, Sarah K. Cotton, Paul S. Steinberg,
Kelly Damphousse, Brent L. Smith

Prepared for the National Memorial Institute for the Prevention of Terrorism

RAND INFRASTRUCTURE, SAFETY, AND ENVIRONMENT

The research described in this report was supported under Award Number MIPT106-113-2000-064 from the National Memorial Institute for the Prevention of Terrorism (MIPT), and the Office for Domestic Preparedness, U.S. Department of Homeland Security (DHS).

Library of Congress Cataloging-in-Publication Data

When terrorism hits home : how prepared are state and local law enforcement? / Lois M. Davis ... [et al.].
p. cm.
"MG-104."
"Supported under award number MIPT106-113-2000-064 from the National Memorial Institute for the Prevention of Terrorism (MIPT) located in Oklahoma City and the Office for Domestic Preparedness, U.S. Department of Homeland Security (DHS)."
Includes bibliographical references.
ISBN 0-8330-3499-5 (pbk. : alk. paper)
1. Terrorism—United States—Prevention—Evaluation. 2. Emergency management—United States—Evaluation. 3. Law enforcement—United States—Evaluation. I. Davis, Lois M.

HV6432.W483 2004
363.32—dc22

2004022721

Cover photo: Getty Images

Published 2004 by the RAND Corporation
1776 Main Street, P.O. Box 2138, Santa Monica, CA 90407-2138
1200 South Hayes Street, Arlington, VA 22202-5050
201 North Craig Street, Suite 202, Pittsburgh, PA 15213-1516
RAND URL: http://www.rand.org/
To order RAND documents or to obtain additional information, contact
Distribution Services: Telephone: (310) 451-7002;
Fax: (310) 451-6915; Email: order@rand.org

Preface

Law enforcement plays a critical role in responding to, preventing, and deterring terrorist attacks. In 1995, on behalf of the U.S. Department of Justice (DOJ), the RAND Corporation conducted a study to assess how prepared state and local law enforcement agencies were for domestic terrorism. In 2002, RAND conducted a follow-up study to assess state and local law enforcement agencies' current preparedness for terrorism in general. The survey was undertaken just prior to the formation of the U.S. Department of Homeland Security (DHS). Thus, it provides an important benchmark for assessing future investments in preparedness. This report presents the results of the 2002 survey for state and local law enforcement agencies conducted one year after the 9/11 attacks and just prior to the formation of DHS.

This nationwide survey of state and local law enforcement was conducted as part of a subcontract to a larger study undertaken by the University of Alabama at Birmingham (more recently by the University of Arkansas) and by the University of Oklahoma to create a national database of American terrorism.

This report should be of interest to policymakers and organizations at the federal, state, and local level involved in emergency preparedness planning, funding, and management.

This research was supported under award number MIPT106-113-2000-064 from the National Memorial Institute for the Prevention of Terrorism (MIPT), located in Oklahoma City, and the Office for Domestic Preparedness (ODP), U.S. Department of Homeland Security (DHS).

This research was conducted within the Homeland Security Program of RAND Infrastructure, Safety, and Environment (ISE), a unit of the RAND Corporation. The mission of ISE is to improve the development, operation, use, and protection of society's essential built and natural assets; and to enhance the related social assets of safety and security of individuals in transit and in their workplaces and communities. The ISE research portfolio encompasses research and analysis on a broad range of policy areas including homeland security, criminal justice, public safety, occupational safety, the environment, energy, natural resources, climate, agriculture, economic development, transportation, information and telecommunications technologies, space exploration, and other aspects of science and technology policy. Inquiries regarding RAND Infrastructure, Safety, and Environment may be directed to:

Debra Knopman, Director
1200 S. Hayes Street
Arlington, VA 22202-5050
Tel: 703.413.1100, extension 5667
Email: ise@rand.org
http://www.rand.org/ise

Points of view in this document are those of the authors and do not necessarily represent the official position of the National Memorial Institute for the Prevention of Terrorism (MIPT) or the U.S. Department of Homeland Security (DHS).

Contents

Figures

Figures

Tables

Summary

Introduction

In 1995, on behalf of the U.S. Department of Justice (DOJ), RAND conducted a study to assess domestic preparedness for terrorism within the United States. That study, which included a nationwide survey, found that state and local law enforcement agencies were lacking in preparedness to respond to domestic terrorism. In particular, it found that there was poor liaison and communication with federal and state officials, little or no training related to terrorism preparedness, little or no intelligence and strategic threat-assessment capability, and minimal expert review of plans and training exercises.

Nearly a decade has passed since the first study was conducted, and a great deal has happened since then in terms of terrorist events occurring on U.S. soil—most prominently the 1995 terrorist attack in Oklahoma City and the September 11, 2001, terrorist attacks on the World Trade Center, the Pentagon, and eastern Pennsylvania.

One consequence of these events was the creation of the Department of Homeland Security (DHS) on November 21, 2002, in legislation signed by President Bush. The concept behind DHS was to unify federal forces and protect our country from a new host of terrorist threats on American soil. Within DHS, the Office for Domestic Preparedness (ODP) is charged with coordinating first-responder terrorism preparedness efforts and working with state and local first responders to improve terrorism preparedness, including training, exercises, and equipment support. ODP is also responsible for directing terrorism preparedness grant programs at the federal level for all emergency response providers and for measuring programmatic performance and improvements in domestic preparedness.

To meet its charge, DHS needs to collect information on first responders and other emergency response providers; such information includes, for example, the challenges first responders have confronted and how they have addressed them. A survey of first and other responders is one of the better ways to help gather such information. As a result, the National Memorial Institute for the Prevention of Terrorism (MIPT, located in Oklahoma City) commissioned the University of Alabama at Birmingham and Oklahoma University to ask RAND to replicate its 1995 study and to reassess and reevaluate current U.S. preparedness for terrorism.

This report presents the results of a 2002 survey conducted one year after the 9/11 attacks and just prior to the formation of DHS, with the goal of assessing how prepared state and local law enforcement agencies currently are for terrorism.[1] In this report, we address five key issues of interest to ODP and DHS: (1) the response experience of law enforcement and threat perceptions; (2) the steps law enforcement has undertaken to counter the threat and to shore up vulnerabilities; (3) law enforcement's support needs; (4) how law enforcement is resourcing preparedness activities; and (5) the relationship between perception of risk, funding, and preparedness.

Law Enforcement's Prior Response Experience and Threat Perceptions

What has been the actual terrorism response experience of law enforcement agencies in the United States? Prior to the 9/11 attacks, few local law enforcement agencies had experience with responding to or investigating a terrorist-related incident. In contrast, state law enforcement agencies before 9/11 had far greater experience, and the ways they had

---

[1] The RAND 2002 nationwide survey was conducted as part of a subcontract to a larger study undertaken by the University of Alabama at Birmingham (and, more recently, by the University of Arkansas) and the University of Oklahoma to create a national database of American terrorism. The larger study is being conducted for MIPT by Dr. Brent Smith and Dr. Kelly Damphousse.

been involved with terrorist-related incidents were more numerous (e.g., assisting with evidence collection, surveillance, and investigations). The 9/11 attacks served to increase the terrorism response experience of both state and local law enforcement agencies. For example, most state law enforcement agencies and about half of local agencies were involved in responding to terrorist-related hoaxes or incidents (primarily anthrax-related) after 9/11. The burden of responding to these incidents was relatively high, particularly for law enforcement agencies located in the large metropolitan counties and for state law enforcement agencies.

What is law enforcement's assessment of the threat to their jurisdiction or state? Half of local law enforcement agencies assessed the chance of a major terrorist incident occurring within their jurisdiction within the next five years as being very low, suggesting that many agencies tend to view preparedness for terrorism as a relatively low priority. Still, one out of five local law enforcement agencies assessed the chance of an attack occurring within their jurisdiction as being somewhat likely or very likely. The types of threats that local law enforcement was most concerned about were those involving the use of chemical or biological agents, conventional explosives, and cyberterrorism. State law enforcement agencies and local law enforcement within large counties, in particular, assessed the chance of such attacks occurring as being relatively high.

What Law Enforcement Is Doing to Counter the Threat and to Shore Up Vulnerabilities

Law Enforcement's Response to 9/11

In response to 9/11, state law enforcement agencies and local law enforcement (particularly those agencies located in large counties) undertook a number of steps to improve their preparedness for terrorism, including

- increasing the number of personnel doing emergency response planning
- updating response plans (for incidents related to chemical, biological, or radiological [CBR] attacks) and, to a lesser degree, mutual aid agreements

- internally reallocating resources or increasing departmental spending to focus on terrorism preparedness.

In addition, most state law enforcement agencies and many local agencies (especially those within large counties) received guidance from the Federal Bureau of Investigation (FBI) about what type of information they should collect and pass on about suspected terrorist activities.

The 9/11 terrorist attacks, along with U.S. domestic preparedness programs, help served as catalysts for increasing assessment activities, particularly at the local level. Before 9/11, state law enforcement agencies and local agencies in large counties had been proactive in conducting risk or threat assessments. Following 9/11, those agencies that had not done so worked to catch up. For example, whereas only a quarter of law enforcement agencies within smaller counties had conducted an assessment before 9/11, nearly three-quarters did so in the year following the 9/11 terrorist attacks.

The majority of state law enforcement agencies and a quarter of local law enforcement had specialized terrorism units. Those agencies with such units were proactive in conducting joint training exercises after 9/11. Law enforcement agencies that lacked specialized terrorism units, in general, were less actively engaged in training activities, suggesting that special attention may be needed toward engaging them more in training.

Variation in Law Enforcement's Approach to Preparedness

The survey results showed variation in law enforcement's approach to preparedness. In general, state law enforcement agencies and local law enforcement agencies in large counties were more proactively engaged in terrorism preparedness activities along its different dimensions (planning, training, etc.) than were law enforcement agencies in smaller counties. This finding is consistent with the higher threat perceptions of these agencies and the higher priority that they assigned to investing departmental resources on terrorism preparedness.

In smaller counties, interagency task forces appear to play a more central role in terms of planning, assessment, and training activities. For example, responsibility for developing contingency plans for terrorism at the state level and in large counties rested primarily with law enforcement, whereas in smaller counties, interagency task forces also shared this responsibility. In terms of assessment activities, even before 9/11, many state law enforcement agencies and local law enforcement agencies within large counties had been proactive in doing risk or threat assessments, with assessment activities at the state level and within large counties being more comprehensive and primarily the responsibility of law enforcement. In comparison, only a quarter of law enforcement agencies in smaller counties had conducted an assessment before 9/11. In smaller counties, assessments tended to be narrow in scope (focusing mostly on public buildings and key infrastructure) and the responsibility of an interagency task force in a number of instances.

In terms of training, in 2002 the Joint Terrorism Task Forces (JTTFs) were an oft-cited source of counterterrorism-awareness training at the local level, particularly for those law enforcement agencies located within large counties. Most law enforcement agencies in large counties and a quarter of those in smaller counties have interacted with the JTTFs, primarily to receive counterterrorism training. Our survey results also indicated relatively modest levels of participation in federally sponsored training programs by local law enforcement. Then again, few state law enforcement agencies reported receiving counterterrorism training from the JTTFs, and these agencies participated more in federally sponsored training programs, suggesting that the JTTFs were not an important source of training for state-level organizations. Given the increased number of training courses being offered since 9/11, the degree of reliance on the JTTFs for counterterrorism training may lessen over time as more and more local law enforcement agencies participate in other training opportunities.

Variation by Size of County

What is typical of the response experience of law enforcement agencies in large counties versus smaller counties, and in what ways do they differ? In general, law enforcement agencies within large counties were more proactive in addressing terrorism preparedness than those located in smaller counties. Consistent with their higher threat perceptions, law enforcement agencies in large counties, for example, were more likely to have

- increased the number of personnel assigned to do emergency response planning following 9/11

- created specialized terrorism units and had those units participate in joint training after 9/11
- conducted risk or threat assessments before 9/11
- had more prior experience in responding to and assisting with terrorist-related investigations and in coordinating with the FBI and other federal agencies.

Law enforcement agencies in large counties were also more likely to be responsible for developing contingency plans and conducting assessments for their jurisdictions.

In contrast, law enforcement agencies in smaller counties were less proactive in improving their preparedness. Consistent with their lower threat perceptions, these agencies were less likely to have

- had experience in coordinating with the JTTFs, the FBI, or with other federal agencies
- received guidance from the FBI following 9/11 as to what information to collect and pass on about the terrorist threat
- made organizational changes to improve their terrorism response capabilities.

Law enforcement agencies in smaller counties also had fewer support needs and were less likely to view improving communications interoperability as an important need.

Law Enforcement's Support Needs

To Improve Assessment Capabilities

Although many state and local law enforcement agencies conducted risk or threat assessments between 2000 and 2002 (either as part of U.S. domestic preparedness programs or in response to 9/11), most expressed a desire for some type of support to help them conduct future assessments. However, what they considered to be their most important support need in this area differed.

Nearly half of state law enforcement agencies and a third of local law enforcement agencies in large counties desired better intelligence information about the terrorist threat or capability, consistent with their higher threat perceptions. In comparison, few law enforcement agencies located in smaller counties desired this type of support. Instead, many agencies in smaller counties considered protocols for conducting or evaluating assessments as being their most important support need, as did a third of state law enforcement agencies.

Training on how to conduct assessments was the most important support need for a third of local law enforcement agencies (in both large and small counties). However, none of the state law enforcement agencies listed training in doing assessments as an important support need, perhaps reflecting the fact that responsibility for doing such assessments tends to fall primarily on localities, with state government's role being more to "roll up" local assessment results into a statewide assessment.

To Strengthen Response Capabilities

The type of support needed to strengthen response capabilities fell into three broad categories: training needs, equipment needs, and other types of support needs. In general, state law enforcement agencies and local law enforcement agencies in large counties tended to have a greater number of support needs, consistent with their higher threat perceptions and their more proactive engagement in preparedness activities. In comparison, law enforcement agencies in smaller counties tended to have fewer support needs, again consistent with their lower threat perceptions and less-active engagement in preparedness activities.

To improve response capabilities, training was a particularly important support need for state law enforcement agencies and local law enforcement located within large counties. Two-thirds of state law enforcement agencies desired more training on conducting joint operations and tabletop or field exercises. Half also desired training on how to operate in a hazardous environment, and a third desired training on evidence collection and the use of the incident command system.

At the local level, nearly half of local law enforcement agencies wanted more joint operational training in preparing for and responding to terrorist-related incidents. Local law enforcement agencies also desired training on evidence collection, how to conduct tabletop or field exercises, and how to operate in hazardous environments. One out of five local law enforcement agencies also desired training on the use of the incident command system. Law enforcement agencies in large counties, in particular, indicated a greater need for training in each of these areas than did law enforcement agencies in smaller counties.

With respect to equipment needs, about half of state and local law enforcement agencies desired support to purchase Level A or B personal protective equipment (PPE) for their response personnel and training on its usage. Consistent with their desire for training on how to operate in hazardous environments and for more and better PPE, a third of local law enforcement and two-thirds of state law enforcement agencies also wanted better sensor technology to rapidly identify hazards that their response personnel may encounter.

Manpower shortfalls appeared to be more acute at the state level. The majority of state law enforcement agencies indicated a need for more manpower to enable them to dedicate personnel to response planning and counterterrorism activities, compared to only a third of local law enforcement agencies.

Within each of the three categories of training, equipment, and other types of support, between two and three times more law enforcement agencies in large counties expressed a need for support than did agencies within smaller counties. Given their higher threat perceptions and their more active engagement in preparedness activities at the local level, this result is not surprising. In addition, law enforcement agencies in large counties were similar to state law enforcement agencies with respect to the proportion of departments that desired more and better intelligence information, support to improve communications interoperability, and training on how to conduct lessons learned and on the use of the incident command system. In other areas, local law enforcement in large counties indicated an even greater need for training and equipment support than state law enforcement, particularly with respect to joint operational training, training on evidence collection and how to operate in hazardous environments, and desire for more and better PPE.

As was true in earlier terrorist incidents, the 9/11 attacks highlighted a number of interoperability problems between first responders involved in multiagency response. RAND's 2002 survey results indicate that many state and local law enforcement agencies continue to have interoperability problems, with two factors—lack of funding and aging communications systems and hardware—being important obstacles to improving interoperability. The majority of state law enforcement agencies and local law enforcement agencies within large counties, in particular, indicated a need to replace aging communications systems and improve communications interoperability. In addition, some state law enforcement agencies and local law enforcement agencies in large counties—that is, those agencies that assess the threat to be greater—cited differences in resource priorities between emergency response agencies as hindering progress in improving interoperability.

Resourcing Preparedness Activities

For many local law enforcement agencies, investing departmental resources on terrorism preparedness was a low priority compared to other agency needs. Although investing such resources was not a high priority, after 9/11, about a quarter of local law enforcement agencies overall (particularly those located in large counties) increased agency spending or internally reallocated resources to focus on terrorism preparedness. They did so for a variety of reasons, including support for planning activities (development of response plans, participation in interagency planning activities) and conducting training and tabletop or field exercises.

We also found a positive correlation between receipt of funding and preparedness activities. Those local law enforcement agencies that received an increase in external funding or resources following 9/11 were more likely than other agencies to have (1) increased spending or internally reallocated resources to focus on terrorism preparedness, (2) updated response plans or standard operating procedures (SOPs) to address terrorist-related incidents (particularly CBR-related), (3) established new mutual aid agreements after 9/11 to address terrorist-related incidents, and (4) conducted joint training exercises after 9/11. These law enforcement agencies were also more likely to have specialized terrorism units and to assign a higher priority to expending departmental resources on terrorism preparedness. Still, only one out of five local law enforcement agencies (regardless of county size) reported receiving external funding (or resources) *from any source* following 9/11 to support their terrorism preparedness activities. The primary sources of support were the federal government or their state's office of emergency management (OEM).

For state law enforcement agencies, investing departmental resources on terrorism preparedness was a higher priority. Following 9/11, half of state law enforcement agencies increased departmental spending, and two-thirds internally reallocated resources to focus on terrorism preparedness. They also did so for a wider variety of reasons than did local law enforcement, including support for interagency planning and coordination activities, developing or modifying response plans, training personnel, establishing specialized terrorism units, and purchasing equipment. Unlike local law enforcement agencies, the majority of state law enforcement agencies received external funding following 9/11, primarily from the federal government. The higher percentage of state law enforcement agencies that received funding after 9/11, as compared to local law enforcement, may partly reflect the shift that occurred from federal grants being distributed directly to the local level now going through the state governments. In addition, some of this funding may have been used by state law enforcement agencies to provide training or to support the planning activities of local law enforcement.

Relationship Between Perception of Risk, Funding, and Preparedness

To better understand the relationship between level of risk, size of jurisdiction, receipt of funding, and preparedness activities, we developed a measure of perceived risk utilizing information from the survey on threat perceptions and on physical vulnerabilities. The results of our analyses are shown in Figure S.1.

Law enforcement agencies that perceived the risk of a future terrorist attack to be higher for their jurisdiction were more likely than other agencies to have (1) updated their response plans or SOPs and mutual aid agreements to address terrorism-related incidents, (2) conducted or participated in joint training exercises with terrorism-related task forces,

Figure S.1.
Identified Relationships Between Perceived Risk, Size of Jurisdiction, Receipt of Funding, and Preparedness Activities

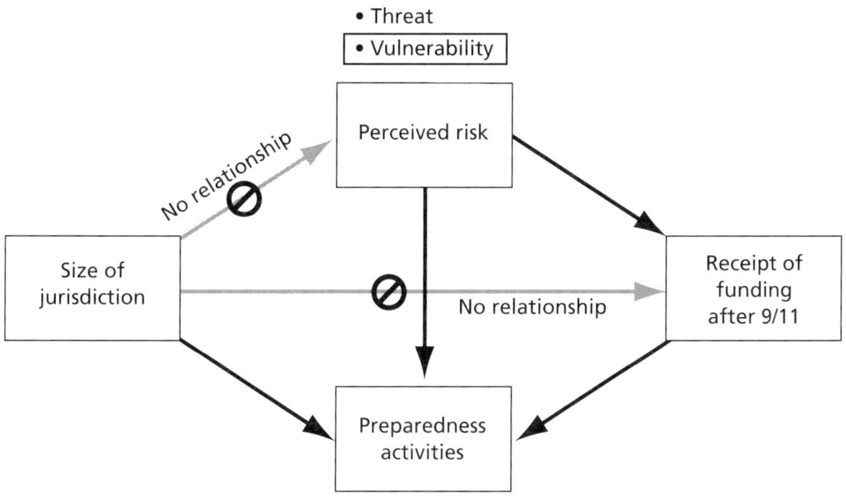

RAND *MG104-S.1*

and (3) internally reallocated departmental resources to focus on improving response capabilities and preparedness for terrorism-related incidents following 9/11. These agencies also tended to assign a higher priority to investing departmental resources on terrorism preparedness and to be proactive in conducting assessments even before 9/11. What appears to be driving our measure of perceived risk was primarily the vulnerability component versus the threat component of risk.[2]

Although size of jurisdiction was predictive of law enforcement undertaking steps to improve their level of preparedness, risk was the better predictor of funding (Figure S.1).[3] That is, law enforcement agencies that assessed the risk to be higher for their jurisdiction were

---

[2] We focused on the vulnerability component versus the threat component of risk because we found no relationship between size of jurisdiction and level of perceived risk (although size of jurisdiction was positively correlated with perception of threat).

[3] That is, law enforcement agencies in large counties tended to be more proactive in addressing terrorism preparedness than were agencies in smaller counties. Law enforcement agencies in large counties also were more likely to assess the threat of future terrorist attacks to be relatively high for their jurisdiction and to assign a higher priority to investing departmental resources on preparedness.

more likely to receive external funding following 9/11 than those that assessed the risk of terrorism to be lower. Size of jurisdiction, on the other hand, was not significantly correlated with receipt of funding. However, the identified associations between level of risk and receipt of funding (and receipt of funding and preparedness activities) do not necessarily imply causal relationships. It may be that law enforcement agencies that perceived the risk of terrorism to be higher for their jurisdiction were, in general, more proactive in seeking funding and more successful at obtaining it. Similarly, law enforcement agencies that were more actively engaged in preparedness activities to begin with may have been more likely to apply for funding following 9/11.

Homeland-security experts and first responders have cautioned against an overemphasis on improving the preparedness of large cities to the exclusion of smaller communities or rural areas, noting that much of our critical infrastructure and some potential high-value targets (nuclear power plants, military installations, agricultural facilities, etc.) are located in less-populated areas. Importantly, we found that perception of risk was not correlated with size of jurisdiction. That is, even law enforcement agencies in smaller counties, if they assessed the risk to be higher for their jurisdiction, were proactive in improving their level of preparedness. The fact that both perceived risk and size of jurisdiction were predictive of undertaking preparedness activities but were not strongly correlated with one another suggests that law enforcement agencies are taking both factors into account.

Conclusions and Future Directions

Law enforcement has played and will continue to play a critical role in responding to, preventing, and deterring terrorist attacks in the United States. As our nation moves forward with efforts to improve U.S. preparedness for terrorism, it is worthwhile to consider the early experiences of law enforcement to see what insights may be gained with respect to their threat perceptions, approach to terrorism preparedness, and what they view as being their critical support needs to inform future programmatic efforts at the local, state, and federal levels.

Conclusions

The survey results have a number of implications for improving programmatic support to the law enforcement community. Consistent with their higher threat perceptions, a majority of state law enforcement agencies and local law enforcement agencies within large counties desired better intelligence information from DHS and DOJ about the threat facing their region or jurisdiction to help strengthen their response capabilities and to inform assessment activities.

Given that law enforcement agencies with specialized terrorism units were more proactive in conducting joint training, DHS may want to direct training funds to these specialized units and support the formation of these units at the local level. Given that law enforcement agencies that lacked specialized terrorism units, in general, tended to be less actively engaged in training activities, ODP and DHS also may want to give special attention toward engaging more of these law enforcement agencies in training activities.

With respect to counterterrorism training, ODP and DHS will want to further consider how to encourage local law enforcement's greater participation in counterterrorism training. One option may be to provide more training resources to the JTTFs. Then again, given the increased demands placed on these task forces since 9/11, it may be difficult for them to take on additional training responsibilities.

Variation in law enforcement's approach to preparedness suggests that future programmatic support at the federal, state, and local levels will need to be tailored to take into account these differences. In addition, any initiative to model or develop objective measures of overall U.S. preparedness for terrorism also will need to take this variation into account. The finding that interagency task forces in smaller counties appear to play a more important role in terms of planning, assessment, coordination, and training activities suggests that these task forces are candidates toward which to direct preparedness funding and training resources.

Variation in law enforcement's support needs to conduct future risk or threat assessments and to strengthen response capabilities suggests that ODP and DHS will want to tailor their programmatic approach to providing support in these areas to take into account this variability in support requirements.

We also identified three areas where there is a need for greater awareness training that DHS may want to address. The first area is the use of PPE.[4] The survey results suggested an incomplete understanding by law enforcement about the purpose of the different levels of PPE and how they relate to the mission(s) of law enforcement when operating in a hazardous-environment situation. The second area is awareness of what counterterrorism training is being offered at the local and state levels. Local law enforcement agencies varied in their awareness of what counterterrorism training was being offered by their police academy or by their state government. The third area of concern is responsibility for developing terrorism contingency plans for a jurisdiction or state. A minority of local law enforcement agencies and state agencies were uncertain who had this responsibility.

Problems with communications interoperability remain a concern. These results suggest that coordinating system planning and acquisition initiatives between multiple response organizations, particularly within the large counties and at the state level, will be important for DHS to focus on. Also, as states and local jurisdictions move forward with replacing aging communications systems and addressing barriers to interoperability, DHS needs to monitor how much such states and jurisdiction are adhering to the detailed guidance on the future technology requirements for public safety communications systems and for interoperability recently put forth by DHS.

In terms of resourcing preparedness activities, the survey results raise the question of what sort of public safety activities may have been sacrificed as a result of shifting resources or personnel to focus on terrorism

---

[4] ODP, as an entity of DOJ under the Office of Justice Programs (OJP) prior to the creation of DHS, administered the 2001 equipment grant program. These were direct grants (not reimbursement) for planning, training, equipment, and exercises. Many of the initial orders for PPE occurred as part of the Fiscal Year 2001 equipment grant program process.

preparedness and response. One can make the argument that emergency preparedness for terrorism may go hand in hand with law enforcement's other public safety duties. Thus, it may be that nothing in the system gave. Yet these results suggest that in taking on these additional demands, some local departments may have been stretched thin during that first year after 9/11. And given economic conditions at the local and state levels and delays in the distribution and spending of federal first-responder grant funds, the question remains a valid concern. DHS will want to monitor and assess the degree to which this may be the case as first-responder funding begins to reach more and more localities.

We were able to show that perceived risk is predictive of law enforcement undertaking steps to improve their preparedness and is a predictor of receipt of funding. Importantly, we found that perception of risk was not correlated with size of jurisdiction, and that law enforcement agencies appear to be taking both factors into account.

A criticism of the statewide assessment process has been that in the past, the formula for distributing first-responder grant funds has not taken into account differences in threat levels between localities. The 2003 statewide assessment process conducted by DHS was intended to gather information on differences in threat levels to help guide future resource-allocation decisions. However, the timeline for completing the assessments was compressed, and there were reported inconsistencies across the states in how the assessments were conducted. Our measures of perceived risk and perceived threat could be used to help validate those assessments.

Finally, future trends in law enforcement's evolving intelligence function suggest that overcoming impediments to information sharing and coordination is important to achieve. Also, the role and function of these specialized terrorism or criminal intelligence units and the intelligence training law enforcement personnel receive will be important for DHS and DOJ to monitor.

Future Directions

Given the timing of the survey, these results provide important baseline information about where the law enforcement community stood on the eve of the formation of DHS and prior to the receipt of substantial federal preparedness funding since 9/11. Extending the survey would provide DHS and other federal departments with a unique opportunity to gauge the progress of their programs in improving terrorism preparedness and in meeting programmatic goals for supporting state and local responders, and to assess how current federal preparedness grant programs are making a difference and where there is room for improvement. In addition, making the survey longitudinal and expanding its focus to include all first-responder organizations (e.g., fire service, emergency medical services, emergency management) would enable DHS to gain a comprehensive picture of how first responders are addressing terrorism preparedness at the state and local levels and, collectively, what that means in terms of overall U.S. preparedness for terrorism.

Acknowledgments

The content of this report has been informed by the contributions of a number of colleagues. In particular, we would like to acknowledge the careful review and insightful comments received from Bruce Don, Michael Grossman, and Brian Houghton on an earlier draft of this report. Henry Willis of RAND also provided valuable input on the development of the risk measure. We also acknowledge the support of this research and the valuable feedback on the preliminary survey findings received from Dennis Reimer and Brian Houghton of the National Memorial Institute for the Prevention of Terrorism (MIPT) in Oklahoma City. Last, but not least, we especially would like to thank the law enforcement agencies that willingly participated in this important survey and provided information about their approach to, and support needs for, ensuring state and local preparedness for terrorism.

Abbreviations

ATF	Bureau of Alcohol, Tobacco, Firearms, and Explosives
ATTF	Anti-Terrorism Task Force
CATI	computer-assisted telephone interviewing
CBR	chemical, biological, or radiological
CBRN	chemical, biological, radiological, or nuclear
CBRNE	chemical, biological, radiological, nuclear, or explosives
COPS	Community Oriented Police Services
DEA	Drug Enforcement Administration
DHHS	U.S. Department of Health and Human Services
DHS	U.S. Department of Homeland Security
DoD	U.S. Department of Defense
DOE	U.S. Department of Energy
DOJ	U.S. Department of Justice
DPP	Domestic Preparedness Program
EMS	emergency medical services
FAA	Federal Aviation Administration
FBI	Federal Bureau of Investigation
FEMA	Federal Emergency Management Agency
FY	fiscal year
GAO	General Accounting Office
HAZMAT	hazardous materials
INS	Immigration and Naturalization Service
JTTFs	Joint Terrorism Task Forces

MIPT	National Memorial Institute for the Prevention of Terrorism
NIJ	National Institute of Justice
NLD	Nunn-Lugar-Domenici
NPSIB	National Public Safety Information Bureau
NTD	National Terrorism Database
ODP	Office for Domestic Preparedness
OEM	Office of Emergency Management
OJP	Office of Justice Programs, U.S. Department of Justice
OSLDPS	Office of State and Local Domestic Preparedness Support
PPE	personal protective equipment
SCBA	self-contained breathing apparatus
SDPEP	State Domestic Preparedness Equipment Program
SDPP	State Domestic Preparedness Program
SHSAS	State Homeland Security Assessment and Strategy
SHSGP	State Homeland Security Grant Program
SLATT	State and Local Anti-Terrorism Training
SOP	standard operating procedure
SRG	Survey Research Group
TEWG	Terrorism Early Warning Group
TTIC	Terrorist Threat Integration Center
UASI	Urban Area Security Initiative
UAWG	Urban Area Working Group
WMD	weapons of mass destruction

CHAPTER ONE

Introduction

Background

In 1995, on behalf of the U.S. Department of Justice (DOJ), the RAND Corporation conducted a study to assess domestic preparedness for terrorism within the United States.[1] That study, which included a nationwide survey along with some case studies, found that state and local law enforcement agencies were unprepared to respond to the threat of terrorism. In particular, it found that there was poor liaison and communication with federal and state officials, little or no training related to terrorism preparedness, little or no intelligence and strategic threat-assessment capability, and minimal expert review of plans and training exercises.

At the time of the original study, although the United States was the country most frequently targeted abroad by terrorists, it was somewhere near the bottom of the list in terms of the number of terrorist attacks annually recorded within its own borders.[2] The bombing of New York's World Trade Center in 1993 was the first time since 1986 that persons (six individuals) had died as a result of a terrorist incident within the United States,[3] and it underscored the fact that the threat of terrorism in this country could not be discounted. This was the situation in the United States when that initial assessment was done.

---

[1] For more details on the study, see K. J. Riley and B. Hoffman, *Domestic Terrorism: A National Assessment of State and Local Preparedness*, Santa Monica, Calif.: RAND Corporation, MR-505-NIJ, 1995.

[2] Riley and Hoffman, 1995.

[3] Riley and Hoffman, 1995.

Nearly a decade has passed since the first study and its survey were conducted, and since then, several terrorist events have occurred on U.S. soil, most prominently the 1995 bombing of the Alfred P. Murrah Federal Building in Oklahoma City, which killed 168 people, and the September 11, 2001, attacks on the World Trade Center, the Pentagon, and eastern Pennsylvania, where many more individuals died. These events brought home the reality of terrorism to the American people. The subsequent anthrax attacks in October 2001 further drove home the potential vulnerability the United States faced from the threat of terrorism.

One consequence of those events was the creation of the U.S. Department of Homeland Security (DHS) on November 21, 2002, in legislation signed by President Bush. The concept behind DHS was to unify federal forces and protect our country from a new host of terrorist threats on American soil. All told, DHS, which entailed the most sweeping government reorganization since World War II, consolidated more than 22 federal agencies.

Within DHS, the Office for Domestic Preparedness (ODP) is charged with coordinating first-responder terrorism preparedness efforts and working with state and local first responders to improve terrorism preparedness, including training, exercises, and equipment support.[4] ODP is also responsible for directing terrorism preparedness grant programs at the federal level for all emergency response providers and for measuring programmatic performance and improvements in domestic preparedness.

To meet its charge, DHS needs to collect information on first responders and other emergency response providers; such information includes, for example, the challenges first responders have confronted and how they have addressed them and their support needs. A survey of first responders is one of the better ways to help gather such information. As a result, the National Memorial Institute for the Prevention of Terrorism (MIPT, located in Oklahoma City)[5] commissioned the

---

[4] The ODP within DHS was formerly located within the DOJ. In March 2003, ODP was transferred from DOJ to the National Memorial Institute for the Prevention of Terrorism.

[5] As part of MIPT's charter of preventing terrorism or mitigating its effects, the foundation sponsors research to help inform the first-responder community—law enforcement, fire service, emergency medical services, and others—on ways to improve their planning, equipping, training, and preparedness in general for terrorism.

University of Alabama at Birmingham and Oklahoma University to ask RAND to replicate its 1995 study and to reassess and reevaluate current U.S. preparedness for terrorism.

Objective

This report addresses five key issues of interest to ODP and DHS: (1) the response experience of law enforcement and their threat perceptions; (2) the steps law enforcement has undertaken to counter the threat and shore up vulnerabilities; (3) law enforcement's support needs; (4) how law enforcement is resourcing preparedness activities; and (5) the relationship between perception of risk, funding, and preparedness.

To address these issues, we present in this report the results of a 2002 survey conducted one year after the 9/11 attacks and just prior to the formation of DHS, with the goal of updating that earlier study and assessing how prepared state and local law enforcement agencies are for terrorism.[6] Because the earlier survey was not continued during the intervening years, it is difficult to make strong comparisons between the 1995 and 2002 surveys. Being able to make more comparisons from one period to the next will be critical if we want to understand how responder preparedness for terrorist attacks has improved and for informing DHS's and other federal departments' programmatic approaches for improving domestic preparedness for terrorism. The 2002 survey provides a unique baseline; more frequent readiness assessments could be used to better inform resource-allocation decisions and the targeting of, for example, training and equipment funding to the responder community. The new 2002 survey expands on the earlier study using a newly designed instrument that addresses a broader range of topics.

---

[6] This nationwide survey was conducted as part of a subcontract to a larger study undertaken by the University of Alabama at Birmingham (more recently by the University of Arkansas) and the University of Oklahoma to create a national database of American terrorism. The larger study is being conducted for MIPT by Dr. Brent Smith and Dr. Kelly Damphousse.

Approach

To accomplish our objective, we designed and fielded a survey addressed to state and local law enforcement agencies. Appendix A provides more detail about the survey methodology we used. In this section, we briefly discuss how we designed the survey, selected the samples, fielded the survey (along with response rates), and prepared the survey data for analysis.

Designing the Survey

In collecting information across the two groups, we used a similar format in the survey. The law enforcement survey instrument, which formed the basis of all the survey instruments, contained four sections: (1) threat environment and organizational experience, (2) departmental resources post-9/11, (3) emergency response planning activities, and (4) organizational information. In addition to the four sections, we included several questions at the end of the survey instruments to collect information on the individual completing the survey; we also provided an opportunity for the respondent to share additional, open-ended comments and suggestions on other issues of importance to their organization that the survey had not addressed. Appendix B reproduces the survey instrument for law enforcement agencies.

The survey instruments were designed as a mail survey that would elicit information on the above-listed areas using structured, semistructured, and open-ended questions. For example, for perceptual items, we used Likert scales; for questions requesting information on planning activities, we used checklists; and for questions about ways to improve coordination between the federal, state, and local levels and the organization's level of preparedness and support needs, we used a combination of the above, along with open-ended items.

Once the initial draft instrument was ready, the surveys were reviewed and pretested to refine and test the draft questionnaire. Individuals pretesting the surveys were experts in each survey field—e.g., law enforcement. Survey instruments were then revised according to feedback from each reviewer. This process of instrument construction was essential in helping us pinpoint and fix instrument problems, streamline questions, and reduce respondent burden.

Selecting the Samples

At the state level, we surveyed a census of state law enforcement agencies in each of the 50 states and used a finite population correction to derive the standard errors for these organizations.

Only the local organizations—in this case, the local law enforcement agencies, the targeted law enforcement sample, and harbor and airport police—required a sampling design. For the local law enforcement agencies, we used the National Public Safety Information Bureau (NPSIB) database to select our sample. Replicating the methodology used in the 1995 Riley and Hoffman RAND study, we used a two-stage sampling design, first selecting counties and then law enforcement agencies within those counties. We used a three-step process for selecting counties in the first stage, selecting (1) 16 counties considered to be potential terrorist targets; (2) the 3 most populous counties within each of four census regions (subject to the constraint that no 2 counties come from the same state, and allowing the previously mentioned 16 counties to be considered for selection), yielding 7 more counties; and (3) 36 more counties from the four census regions by three categories of population size: counties with a population greater than 500,000, counties with a population between 100,000 and 500,000, and counties with a population less than 100,000. In total, the three-step process yielded 59 counties in the sample.

The second stage of sampling was to select local law enforcement agencies within each of the 59 counties to survey. First, we identified for each county the municipal or county law enforcement agency of the county seat and included them in the sample. Then we stratified the remaining law enforcement agencies within the county by departmental size and randomly selected one agency from each of the three strata. We defined small departments as those having fewer than 31 officers, medium as having 31 to 100 officers, and large as having more than 100 officers. In smaller and/or rural counties, we expected that the number of law enforcement agencies would constrain our ability to sample agencies in each of the departmental-size strata. We selected

107 agencies based on the county seat, and 104 agencies were randomly sampled, for a total of 211 local law enforcement agencies.

To select the targeted sample of local law enforcement agencies, our initial plan was to identify local jurisdictions that had *experienced* a terrorist incident that resulted in an indictment between 1995 and 2003 (as defined by the Federal Bureau of Investigation [FBI] and inclusion in the National Terrorism Database [NTD]). Approximately 50 jurisdictions have experienced terrorist attacks during these years, with some states experiencing multiple incidents. The attacks include notorious incidents such as the bombing of the Alfred P. Murrah Federal Building in Oklahoma City, as well as less-publicized incidents such as bombings of abortion clinics and militia activities.

The FBI files that contained information on indictments from September 1998 to the present were not available to the project leaders in time for us to use this source to complete our drawing of the sample of law enforcement agencies in jurisdictions that had terrorist acts that led to an indictment. Therefore, the targeted sample only contains law enforcement agencies from each of the jurisdictions for which we had data for the period from January 1995 to August 1998. This resulted in a sample of 37 law enforcement agencies.

We also drew a purposeful sample of 29 harbor and airport law enforcement agencies in major metropolitan areas and port cities.

Fielding the Survey

The data collection process was conducted through a mail survey (with telephone follow-up), with individually crafted questions for each responder population. The primary components involved in fielding the survey were as follows:

- an advance letter from the RAND principal investigator
- the survey packet itself, which contained a cover letter from MIPT, the survey booklet, and a commemorative "Preventing Terrorism" pen used as a response incentive[7]

---

[7] F. Fowler, Jr., *Survey Research Methods,* 2nd ed., Newbury Park, Calif., Sage Publications, 1993.

- telephone follow-up to ensure arrival of the survey and to emphasize the importance of the study
- the establishment of a toll-free 800 number to field respondent questions
- follow-up postcard reminders mailed two weeks after the initial survey mailing
- the mailing of a second, replacement survey
- the final round of telephone follow-up.

Table 1.1 shows the final response rates. Overall, we achieved a high response rate for state and local law enforcement. The response rate was 81 percent for local law enforcement organizations and 78 percent for state law enforcement organizations.

Preparing the Data for Analysis

In preparing the data for analysis, we needed to conduct survey weighting for the local law enforcement sample to adjust for our sampling design and for nonresponse. We did not need to reweight the state law enforcement survey, since we found that the nonresponse rates did not vary by factors that we thought could affect an organization's decision to respond to the survey (region, population size, etc.).

Table 1.1
Final Survey Response Rates

Response Organizations	Number of Organizations Surveyed	Number of Organizations Responding	Response Rate (%)
Local Organizations			
Local law enforcement	209[a]	169	81
Targeted law enforcement	37	29	78
Harbor and airport law enforcement	29	15	52
State Organizations			
State law enforcement	50	39	78
Total/Overall Rate	325	252	78

[a]Two counties were ineligible for inclusion in survey.

For the law enforcement sample, survey weights were calculated to take into account differences in each local law enforcement agency's probability of being selected into the sample and for nonresponse. By weighting each organization during the analysis, we could make inferences about all local law enforcement agencies in the nation. Each organization's survey weight can be expressed as the probability that a given agency in a given county in a region was selected and completed the survey. This probability is the product of three parts, where the first part is the probability that a given county was selected; the second part is the probability that a given agency was selected, given that a given county was selected; and the third part is the probability that the given agency responded to the survey, given that the agency was selected.

The third part accounts for the fact that certain agencies may be more likely to respond to the survey than others. We hypothesized that region, county size, and department size may affect how likely an organization was to respond. The only difference that we observed was that organizations in the West were significantly more likely to respond than organizations in other regions. The response probabilities for each region were Northeast, 0.66; Midwest, 0.72; South, 0.82; and West, 0.85.

Limitations

As is true of survey research in general, there are several important study limitations that the reader should keep in mind. First, the study focus is at the organizational level. However, we recognize that the survey responses depend on how informed a particular individual is about his or her organization's experiences with terrorism preparedness in general and with his or her organization's emergency response and planning activities. Since an individual is responding for an entire organization, we attempted to control for this by asking the organizational head to designate who within their organization would be most informed about emergency preparedness activities related to terrorism. To the extent that individuals who completed the survey for their organization differed in their level of knowledge about their organization's experience in this area, the responses received may partly reflect true differences between organizations or differences in the knowledge and experience of respondents about their organization.

Second, as noted above, the study investigated systematic nonresponse and accounted for nonresponse patterns evident in the background variables available in the construction of the sampling frame. However, other sources of nonresponse may exist, possibly causing biases unaccounted for herein.

Third, since this survey was conducted just following the anniversary of the September 11 attacks, one might expect that respondents may be more sensitized to the issue of terrorism and emergency preparedness for such incidents. It is difficult to predict the direction of any bias because of a heightened sensitivity to this issue. For example, one can argue that heightened sensitivity may lead to some individuals understating the level of preparedness of their organization—that is, the more you know, the more likely you are to assess your organization as being less prepared. Then again, individuals who are less sensitized to this issue may be more likely to overstate their organization's level of preparedness. We suspect that the direction and magnitude of the bias resulting from this sensitivity will differ for objective versus subjective measures.

Fourth, in interpreting these results, it is important to keep in mind that much has changed since the original 1995 study, where distinct structures at the state level did not exist to specifically address homeland security and preparedness. For one thing, the role and responsibilities of state law enforcement organizations vary considerably from state to state, ranging from highway patrol to a wider public safety role. Thus, it is important to keep in mind that these organizations may serve different functions. Further, a number of states have a public safety department established under which law enforcement is just one component. Within that department, emergency management may be the lead state-level organization for terrorism preparedness, or it may fall to a state interagency task force or to the state's Office of Homeland Security. Since the September 11 attacks, states have reorganized emergency response functions to specifically address terrorism, and states vary in terms of which organization or entity has been assigned the lead role of ensuring their state's preparedness for terrorism and within which agency their state Office of Homeland Security resides, ranging from state offices of emergency management (OEMs), state public safety departments, and state law enforcement agencies to interagency coordinating councils or task forces or placement directly within the governor's office.[8] In addition, the FBI has been designated as the lead agency on terrorist investigations, with state and local police providing a supporting role.

Organization of This Report

We organize the findings in this report in four chapters. Chapter Two describes law enforcement's actual response experience with terrorism in the United States and law enforcement's assessment of the threat facing their jurisdiction or state. Chapter Three presents the survey results on what preparedness activities state and local law enforcement agencies have undertaken to counter the threat of terrorism and to shore up vulnerabilities. Chapter Four presents the survey results on what state and local law enforcement view as being their important support needs and how law enforcement agencies are resourcing their preparedness activities. Chapter Five examines in depth the relationship between perception of risk, size of jurisdiction, preparedness activities, and receipt of funding. Chapter Six provides some conclusions and discusses the policy implications of these results and future directions.

Appendix A contains a further discussion of our survey methodology. Appendix B contains a discussion of the analysis of perceived threat and characteristics of law enforcement agencies.

---

[8] For a listing of state offices of homeland security and a brief summary of their missions and relevant legislation, see National Legislative Services and Security Association, homepage, http://www.ncsl.org/programs/legman/nlssa/sthomelandoffcs.htm (as of January 7, 2004).

CHAPTER TWO

Response Experience of Law Enforcement Agencies with Terrorism

What has been law enforcement's actual response experience with terrorism in the United States? What is law enforcement's assessment of the threat to their jurisdiction or state? The 2002 survey was designed to collect information about state and local law enforcement agencies' prior experience in responding to or helping to investigate terrorist-related incidents. We also asked about what types of physical vulnerabilities are located within their jurisdiction or region. Lastly, we asked about their perceptions of terrorist threats facing their jurisdiction or state and the likelihood of future attacks occurring. Their answers are informative about law enforcement agencies' experience with terrorism to date and the types of threats they are focusing on to address preparedness.

Analytic Approach

Using the survey data, we conducted descriptive analyses presenting the weighted results in order to represent the national estimate of local law enforcement agencies—an estimate that accounts for our sample design and for nonresponse bias. For state law enforcement agencies, no weighting was necessary since we undertook a census of these organizations. We used a finite population correction to derive the standard errors for the state-level organizations. (See the discussions in Chapter One and Appendix A.)

In addition, where the differences are significant, we present the results for local law enforcement both overall and by size of county.

Specifically, we make comparisons between law enforcement agencies located in large metropolitan counties (i.e., central counties of metropolitan areas with a population of 1 million or more)[1] and law enforcement agencies located in smaller counties (i.e., counties with a population of less than 1 million). For ease of reference, we have labeled these comparisons in the tables as *metro* versus *non-metro.*

Few Local Law Enforcement Agencies Had Prior Experience with Terrorism

The newly created MIPT American Terrorism Study Database cataloged a total of 121 federal terrorism cases between 1978 and 1999.[2] Specifically, the database contains information on federal terrorist investigations that actually resulted in federal indictments. The FBI investigates far more criminal acts as potential terrorist incidents than it actually classifies as such.[3] From the original RAND 1995 study and the 2002 survey, we know that law enforcement officials tend to consider a wider range of issues and activities to be terrorist-related acts as compared to the FBI, which uses a more restrictive definition of terrorism. As was true in the 1995 study, here we use the term *terrorist-related* to reflect the perspective of the law enforcement respondents to our 2002 survey. That is, these agencies are reporting on what they perceive as being potential terrorist-related incidents or investigations. However, when considering the following survey results, it is important to keep in mind that their perceptions may not necessarily reflect the perspective of the FBI or other federal agencies.

In the 2002 survey, state and local law enforcement agencies were asked what types of terrorist groups were located within their jurisdic-

---

[1] Definition is based on the Office of Research and Planning, Bureau of Health Professions, Area Resource File, 2000.

[2] MIPT, "Terrorism Indictment Database: Researchers Release Terrorism Database to Scholars Nationwide," Oklahoma City, November 20, 2003. Online at http://www.mipt.org/Terrorism-Indictment-Database.asp (as of January 15, 2003).

[3] K. J. Riley and B. Hoffman. *Domestic Terrorism: A National Assessment of State and Local Preparedness,* Santa Monica, Calif.: RAND Corporation, MR-505-NIJ, 1995.

tion or state. In general, most state law enforcement agencies noted the presence of potential terrorist groups[4] within their state. However, only one out of five local law enforcement agencies indicated awareness that such groups were present within their jurisdiction (Table 2.1).

Prior to the 9/11 attacks, few local law enforcement agencies had experience with responding to or investigating terrorist-related incidents. Most local law enforcement agencies (88 percent) reported that no terrorist-related incidents had occurred within their jurisdiction within the past five years (Table 2.2). Only 10 percent of local agencies reported between one and five incidents attributable to a terrorist group had occurred within their jurisdiction (Table 2.2). Of those

Table 2.1
What Potential Terrorist Groups Are Located Within Their Jursidiction or State

Type of Group	All State LE Orgs. (%)	All Local LE Orgs. (%)
Right-wing	85 (3)	17 (5)
Race/ethnicity/hate-related	82 (3)	19 (6)
Religious groups utilizing violence	38 (4)	3 (1)
Single-issue/special-interest	74 (3)	24 (7)
Millennial/doomsday cults	8 (2)	3 (3)
Other	15 (3)	7 (4)

Standard error of the estimate shown in parentheses.

Table 2.2
Frequency of Incidents in Past 5 Years Attributed to Terrorist Group(s)

Number of Incidents in Past Five Years Attributed to Terrorist Group(s)	Within Their Jurisdiction, All Local LE Orgs. (%)	Within Their State, All State LE Orgs. (%)
1–5	10 (4)	35 (4)
6–10	1 (0.5)	14 (3)
11–15	0.4 (0.2)	8 (2)
16–20	0.1 (0.1)	3 (1)
+21	0.4 (0.4)	8 (2)
None	88 (4)	32 (4)

Standard error of the estimate shown in parentheses.

---

[4] Right-wing, race/ethnicity/hate-related, or single-issue/special-interest groups.

agencies that reported such an occurrence, the primary ways in which their department had been involved with such incidents was in terms of being placed on alert, being asked to provide information, or assisting with an investigation (Table 2.3).

By comparison, state law enforcement agencies tended to have greater awareness of and experience with terrorist-related incidents before 9/11. The frequency of reported incidents by state law enforcement agencies for their state was much higher during the same five-year period. For example, 35 percent of state law enforcement agencies said 1–5 incidents had occurred within their state that were attributed to terrorist groups; 14 percent reported 6–10 incidents; and 8 percent reported more than 21 incidents (Table 2.2).

Also, the ways in which state law enforcement agencies had been involved in terrorist-related incidents were more numerous (Table 2.3). In addition to providing information or being placed on alert status, about two-thirds of state law enforcement agencies had assisted with investigations, and about half had been involved in surveillance activities. Over a third had assisted with the collection of evidence and/or been involved in the prosecution of cases. The greater experience of

Table 2.3
Prior to 9/11, Ways in Which Law Enforcment Was Involved in Terrorist-Related Incident(s)

Type of Involvement	Local Law Enforcement All Orgs. (%)	State Law Enforcement All Orgs. (%)
Investigation	13 (5)	64 (4)
Surveillance	6 (2)	54 (4)
Asked to provide information	12 (3)	69 (4)
Placed on alert	12 (4)	46 (4)
Prosecution	2 (1)	23 (3)
Collection of evidence	4 (1)	38 (4)
Scientific analysis	2 (1)	23 (3)
Other	2 (1)	13 (3)

Standard error of the estimate shown in parentheses. Respondents were asked to mark all of the categories that applied.

state law enforcement agencies with terrorist-related incidents prior to 9/11 is not surprising given that these agencies have more frequent interactions with the federal government, that the normal process for dealing with such cases flows from the federal to the state to the local levels, and that a number of these incidents and investigations may have crossed both jurisdictional and state boundaries.

Following 9/11, State and Local Law Enforcement Gained More Experience in Responding to Terrorist-Related Incidents

Following 9/11, both state and local law enforcement agencies have gained more experience with responding to terrorist-related incidents or hoaxes. Nearly half of local law enforcement agencies indicated that following 9/11, terrorist-related hoaxes or incidents had occurred within their jurisdiction or region that required a response by their department (Table 2.4). Most of these hoaxes or incidents were related to chemical, biological, or radiological (CBR) attacks (for the most part, anthrax-related).[5] Law enforcement agencies in large (metro) counties were twice as likely as local agencies in smaller (non-metro) counties to have experienced such hoaxes or incidents following 9/11.

Following the 9/11 attacks, anthrax hoaxes or scares were pervasive across the nation. The burden of fielding calls about (and responding to) suspected "white powder" (i.e., anthrax) incidents at the local level was relatively high, particularly for law enforcement agencies in large metropolitan counties. For example, overall, local law enforcement agencies reported that they had responded to 21 white-powder hoaxes or incidents on average during the peak month of such incidents for their jurisdiction following 9/11. In comparison, agencies in large metropolitan counties responded on average to 41 white-powder incidents during the peak month for their jurisdiction (Table 2.4).

[5] In addition to CBR-related incidents, 11 percent of local law enforcement agencies indicated that other types of incidents were involved (e.g., hate crimes, armed assaults, arson, and threats made against Arab-Americans).

Table 2.4
Following 9/11, Did Local Law Enforcement Agencies Experience Terrorist Hoaxes or Incidents?

	All Local LE Orgs. (%)		
Experienced?	**Overall**	**Metro**	**Non-Metro**
Yes	42 (10)	60 (12)	37 (12)

Of Those Agencies That Did, What Type of Incidents Were Involved? (%)

Type of Incident	Overall	Metro	Non-Metro
CBR-related	83 (8)	89 (5)	80 (11)
Military-grade weapons-related	2 (1)	3 (2)	1 (1)
Cyberterrorism-related	2 (1)	4 (2)	0
Agroterrorism-related	2 (1)	2 (2)	2 (2)

Following 9/11, Number of "White Powder" Incidents Local Law Enforcement Agencies Responded to During Peak Month

No. of White-Powder Incidents	Overall (Mean)	Metro (Mean)	Non-Metro (Mean)
Peak month	21 (4)	41 (13)	13 (3)

Standard error of the estimate shown in parentheses. Military-grade weapons refers to automatic weapons, etc. The term "white powder" incidents refer to anthrax hoaxes or actual anthrax-related incidents following 9/11.

Most state law enforcement agencies (90 percent, S.E. 2) reported responding to such hoaxes or threats (mostly anthrax-related) following 9/11. The burden of responding to white-powder hoaxes or incidents also was high for state law enforcement agencies. State agencies responded on average to 390 (S.E. 76) white-powder incidents during the peak month of such incidents for their state (not shown).

The top-mentioned types of targets of these hoaxes and incidents are shown in Table 2.5. At the state and local levels, they included private citizens, businesses or firms, public gathering places, and public officials. In addition, nearly 20 percent of state law enforcement agencies mentioned airports and utilities (power and water), and 11 percent mentioned nuclear power plants. Few local law enforcement agencies

Table 2.5
Following 9/11, What Were the Top-Mentioned Targets of These Terrorist Hoaxes or Incidents?

Targets	Local LE Orgs. That Experienced Hoaxes/ Incidents (%)	State LE Orgs. That Experienced Hoaxes/ Incidents (%)
Private citizens	57 (11)	51 (5)
Private firms or businesses	24 (9)	17 (4)
Public gathering places	17 (9)	20 (4)
Public officials or government reps	11 (7)	31 (4)
Airports	2 (1)	17 (4)
Utilities (power/ water)	10 (7)	17 (4)
Nuclear power plant	0.1 (0.1)	11 (3)
Military personnel or installations	2 (2)	6 (2)
Transportation systems	2 (2)	6 (2)
Banking or financial institutions	1 (1)	6 (2)
Telecommunications systems	1 (1)	0
University/corporate biotechnology research sites	1 (1)	9 (3)
Other	27 (9)	46 (5)

Standard error of the estimate shown in parentheses. Public gathering places includes such places as stadiums, shopping malls, theaters, sports arenas, etc.

mentioned military installations, utilities, telecommunications, or transportation systems—those facilities or infrastructure that some experts consider possible targets and where much emphasis on preparedness has been placed.[6] This result may reflect in part the greater difficulty of gaining access to these facilities or infrastructure or that threats made may not have been reported to local law enforcement (e.g., in the case of military installations).

At the time of our 2002 survey, a majority[7] of state law enforcement agencies reported that there were ongoing investigations of terrorist groups or related incidents within their state. At the local level,

[6] The "Other" category included movie studios, abortion clinics and other health-care facilities, schools, religious institutions, and others (not shown).

[7] 66 percent, standard error 4.

few law enforcement agencies (5 percent, S.E. 2) reported this to be the case (not shown).

Potential Physical Vulnerabilities Vary at the Local Level

We asked law enforcement agencies what types of physical facilities or infrastructure were located within their jurisdiction or state to get at potential vulnerabilities. Specifically, we gave survey respondents a list of candidate facilities and infrastructure and asked them to indicate which were located within their jurisdiction or region. They also were asked to note any other facilities within their jurisdiction or region that their departments might consider potential targets.

Law enforcement agencies varied in the types of facilities or infrastructure within their jurisdiction or region that they considered to be potential targets of future terrorist attacks. At the local level, the most common types of facilities listed were airports and water-treatment plants (Table 2.6).[8] Between 20 and 25 percent of local law enforcement agencies also listed agroterrorism-related facilities (i.e., food-processing and agricultural producing facilities). A similar percentage of local agencies also listed military installations, chemical plants, public transportation networks, and major suspension and arterial bridges.

There were some key differences in the types of facilities listed by law enforcement agencies in large counties versus those located in smaller counties. Law enforcement agencies in large counties were more likely to cite chemical plants (44 percent versus 16 percent), public transportation networks (47 percent versus 18 percent), and university and corporate biotech research sites (27 percent versus 8 percent) as potential targets (Table 2.6).[9] Then again, certain types of facilities were more common in the smaller counties, such as airports, major suspension and arterial bridges, oil refineries and power plants, and hydroelectric dams.

---

[8] We did not distinguish between large or small airports.

[9] The "Other" category shown in Table 2.6 included shopping malls, major hotels and resorts, women's clinics or hospitals, religious institutions, historical landmarks, universities, and national laboratories.

Table 2.6
What Potential Targets for Future Incidents Are Within Local Law Enforcement Agencies' Jurisdiction?

	All Organizations (%)		
Potential Targets	**Overall**	**Metro**	**Non-Metro**
Water-treatment plants	54 (12)	47 (13)	55 (15)
Airports	41 (10)	24 (7)	45 (13)
Food-processing facilities	26 (7)	29 (11)	25 (9)
Agricultural producing facilities	25 (8)	35 (16)	22 (8)
Military installations	21 (7)	19 (7)	22 (8)
Major suspension/arterial bridges	20 (7)	9 (4)	22 (9)
Other public transportation networks	24 (7)	47 (13)	18 (7)
Chemical plants	22 (7)	44 (14)	16 (7)
Major sports arenas or venues	14 (5)	14 (5)	14 (6)
Oil refineries/power plants/oil or gas pipelines	14 (6)	6 (3)	16 (7)
Hydroelectric dams	10 (4)	1 (1)	12 (5)
Major port facilities	9 (5)	6 (3)	9 (6)
Weapons manufacturer or storage	9 (4)	7 (3)	9 (5)
University/corporate biotechnology research sites	12 (4)	27 (9)	8 (4)
DOE Nuclear Facilities (research labs, storage area, production facilities)	5 (3)	8 (4)	4 (3)
Nuclear power plants	5 (3)	3 (1)	5 (3)
Other	22 (7)	61 (12)	13 (6)

Standard error of the estimate shown in parentheses. Other public transport networks include subways, trains, etc.

Most local law enforcement agencies had one or more of the facility types shown in Table 2.6 within their jurisdiction or region. A third of agencies indicated that their jurisdiction had between one and three types of facilities listed in Table 2.6, and 40 percent had four or more types of facilities (Table 2.7). Few law enforcement agencies in the large counties said they had none of the facility types listed in Table 2.6 within their jurisdiction. In comparison, a third of agencies in smaller counties reported having none of the facility types listed in Table 2.6,

Table 2.7
Number of Facility Types Within Jurisdiction

	All Local Law Enforcement Orgs. (%)		
No. of Facility Types Within Jurisdiction	**Overall**	**Metro**	**Non-Metro**
0	27 (14)	4 (3)	32 (17)
1–3	33 (9)	59 (12)	27 (10)
4+	40 (10)	37 (11)	41 (12)

Standard error of the estimate shown in parentheses.

suggesting fewer potential targets (and a lower level of vulnerability) in these less-populated counties.

Although we asked the same question of state law enforcement agencies, the results are not shown here; most indicated that their state had all of the facility types and infrastructure listed in Table 2.6 (with one exception).[10]

Most Local Law Enforcement Agencies Perceive the Threat to Be Low for Their Jurisdiction

A threat assessment is a process by which one can evaluate the likelihood of terrorist activity against a certain asset or location. Such an assessment can be used as a decision support tool to determine what types of threats to prepare for and how to allocate public safety and emergency response resources.[11] We did not undertake a formal assessment as part of this survey effort. Instead, we asked about law enforcement's perceptions regarding the terrorist threat facing their jurisdic-

[10] The exception was U.S. Department of Energy (DOE) nuclear facilities, including research laboratories, production sites, and storage areas. Only a third of state law enforcement agencies reported having such facilities within their state.

[11] U.S. General Accounting Office (GAO), "Homeland Security: Key Elements of a Risk Management Approach," Statement of Raymond J. Decker, Defense Capabilities and Management, Testimony Before the Subcommittee on National Security, Veterans Affairs, and International Relations; House Committee on Government Reform, GAO-02-150T, October 12, 2001.

tion or state. Presumably, their perceptions will be informative as to the types of threats for which they feel it is important for their department to be preparing.

Specifically, we asked survey respondents to rate the likelihood of different types of major terrorist incidents occurring within their jurisdiction or region within the next five years. The types of incidents asked about were CBR, cyberterrorism, conventional-explosives incidents, agroterrorism, and incidents involving the use of military-grade weapons.[12]

Half of local law enforcement agencies considered the chance of a major terrorist incident occurring within their jurisdiction or region within the next five years to be very unlikely (Table 2.8).[13] Still, some agencies did give credence to the possibility of a future terrorist attack occurring. Specifically, one out of five local law enforcement agencies rated the likelihood of an incident occurring that involved the use of conventional explosives, a biological or chemical agent, or cyberterrorism to be somewhat likely to very likely.

In general, law enforcement agencies in larger counties perceived the threat to be somewhat greater for their jurisdiction than did agencies in smaller counties. Although not shown, for each of the types of incidents listed in Table 2.8, law enforcement agencies in large counties rated the likelihood of occurrence to be higher than did agencies in smaller counties. The one exception was for agroterrorism involving animal disease, where both groups of law enforcement agencies rated its likelihood of occurrence similarly.

In comparison, most state law enforcement agencies rated the terrorist threat to be higher than did local law enforcement. For example, three-quarters of state agencies considered the likelihood of a terrorist attack occurring within their state that involved the use of conventional explosives or cyberterrorism to be somewhat likely or very likely (Table

---

[12] Military-grade weapons included automatic weapons, mortars, etc. For each type of incident, respondents were asked to rate the likelihood of that incident occurring in their jurisdiction or region within the next five years on a scale of 1 to 4, where 1 = very unlikely, 2 = somewhat unlikely, 3 = somewhat likely, and 4 = very likely.

[13] The exception was incidents involving the use of conventional explosives; only a quarter of law enforcement agencies rated it to be very unlikely.

Table 2.8
Perceived Likelihood of Different Types of Terrorist Incidents Occuring Within Their Jurisdiction or Region Within the Next Five Years.

	All Local Law Enforcement Orgs. (%)			
Incident Type	Very Unlikely	Somewhat Unlikely	Somewhat Likely	Very Likely
Chemical	54 (11)	29 (8)	13 (5)	4 (3)
Biological	52 (11)	31 (9)	15 (6)	2 (1)
Radiological	53 (11)	38 (10)	8 (4)	1 (1)
Cyberterrorism	51 (11)	28 (8)	18 (6)	3 (1)
Conventional Explosives	26 (9)	55 (11)	17 (6)	2 (1)
Military-grade weapons (e.g., mortars, automatic weapons)	50 (11)	40 (10)	9 (4)	1 (1)
Agroterrorism involving food contaminants	47 (12)	40 (10)	13 (5)	0
Agroterrorism involving animal disease	52 (11)	34 (9)	13 (5)	1

Standard error of the estimate shown in parentheses. Each row adds to 100 percent.

2.9). Also, about half of state agencies considered the likelihood of a chemical incident occurring within their state to be somewhat likely or very likely. Between 40 and 45 of these agencies gave a similar rating of likelihood for the other types of incidents listed in Table 2.9.

Discussion

What has been the actual terrorism response experience of law enforcement agencies in the United States? Prior to the 9/11 attacks, few local law enforcement agencies had experience with responding to or investigating a terrorist-related incident. Of those that had (one out of ten), the primary ways in which their department had been involved with terrorist-related incidents was in terms of being placed on alert, being asked to provide information, or assisting with an investigation.

By contrast, before 9/11, state law enforcement agencies had far greater experience with terrorist-related incidents than had local law

Table 2.9
Perceived Likelihood of Different Types of Terrorist Incidents Occurring Within Their State Within the Next FIve Years

	All State Law Enforcement Orgs. (%)			
Incident Type	Very Unlikely	Somewhat Unlikely	Somewhat Likely	Very Likely
Chemical	23 (3)	23 (3)	33 (4)	21 (3)
Biological	26 (3)	32 (4)	26 (3)	16 (3)
Radiological	18 (3)	40 (4)	29 (3)	13 (3)
Cyberterrorism	0	24 (3)	52 (4)	24 (3)
Conventional Explosives	5 (2)	24 (3)	39 (4)	32 (4)
Military-grade weapons (e.g., mortars, automatic weapons)	23 (3)	31 (4)	36 (4)	10 (2)
Agroterrorism involving food contaminants	10 (2)	44 (4)	38 (4)	8 (2)
Agroterrorism involving animal disease	16 (3)	39 (4)	40 (4)	5 (2)

Standard error of the estimate shown in parentheses. Each row adds to 100 percent.

enforcement. The ways in which state law enforcement agencies had been involved with these incidents also were more numerous. In addition to providing information and being placed on alert status, two-thirds of state law enforcement agencies had assisted with terrorist-related investigations, and about half had been involved in surveillance activities. Over a third had assisted with the collection of evidence, and about a quarter had provided scientific analysis of evidence or been involved in the prosecution of a case. These differences between state and local law enforcement agencies in prior experience with terrorist-related incidents are not surprising given that the normal process for the investigation of these cases goes from the federal to the state to the local levels.

Following 9/11, both state and local law enforcement gained more experience in responding to terrorist-related hoaxes or incidents. The 9/11 attacks also narrowed somewhat prior differences in experience between state and local law enforcement. Most state law enforcement agencies and about half of local agencies were involved in responding to terrorist-related hoaxes or incidents (primarily anthrax-related) after 9/11. The burden of responding to these incidents was relatively high, particularly for law enforcement agencies located in the large metropolitan counties and for state law enforcement agencies. The targets at the state and local levels most commonly cited were private citizens, businesses or firms, public gathering places, or public officials.

In terms of physical vulnerabilities, local law enforcement agencies differed on the types of facilities or infrastructure located within their jurisdiction or region that they considered to be potential targets for future terrorist attacks. Airports and water-treatment plants were the most common types of facilities reported. Law enforcement agencies in large counties also listed such facilities or infrastructure as chemical plants, public transportation networks, and biotechnology research sites, whereas agencies in smaller counties were more likely to list airports, major suspension and arterial bridges, oil refineries, power plants, and hydroelectric dams. Most local law enforcement agencies had one or more of these facility types within their jurisdiction or region.

State law enforcement agencies reported having most of the facility types within their state, with the exception of U.S. Department of Energy (DOE) nuclear facilities (i.e., research laboratories, production sites, or storage areas). Only a third of state law enforcement agencies reported having DOE nuclear facilities within their state.

One year after the 9/11 attacks, what was law enforcement's assessment of the threat to their jurisdiction or state? At the local level, about half of law enforcement agencies assessed the chance of a major terrorist incident occurring within their jurisdiction within the next five years as being very low. Still, one out of five agencies assessed the likelihood of a terrorist attack occurring within their jurisdiction as somewhat likely or very likely, suggesting that these agencies are more likely to be proactive in improving their level of preparedness. At the local level, the types of threats law enforcement was most concerned about were those involving the use of chemical or biological agents, conventional explosives, and cyberterrorism.

One of the questions of interest to ODP is whether jurisdictions of different sizes and threat levels should be prepared at the same level. We found that law enforcement agencies in large counties assessed the likelihood of different types of threats as being somewhat higher for their jurisdictions as compared to those located in smaller counties.

The higher threat perceptions of these law enforcement agencies suggests that they may be more proactive in improving their overall level of preparedness than those agencies located in smaller counties.

In general, law enforcement agencies at the state level tended to perceive the threat to be higher than did local law enforcement. Nearly three-quarters of state law enforcement agencies assessed the chance of a cyberterrorist attack or of a conventional-explosives attack occurring within their state during the next five years as being somewhat likely or very likely. At least half of state agencies also considered the occurrence of a chemical incident to be somewhat likely or very likely. Between 40 and 45 percent of state agencies assessed the likelihood of biological, conventional-explosives, or agroterrorist-related incidents occurring as being somewhat likely or very likely.

The threat perceptions of law enforcement agencies are informative in terms of what types of terrorist threats law enforcement considers to be more likely to occur and, thus, what types of threats they view as being important for their department to be preparing for. The next chapter describes the steps undertaken by state and local law enforcement to improve their overall preparedness for such terrorist acts.

CHAPTER THREE

Preparedness Results for Law Enforcement Agencies

In the original 1995 RAND study of state and local preparedness for terrorism, RAND researchers noted that prior to the February 1993 bombing of the World Trade Center, most Americans regarded terrorism as something that happened elsewhere.[1] However, since then, much has changed, and the nature of the terrorist threat has continuously evolved. As summarized by Bruce Hoffman, one of the authors of the original 1995 study and a leading terrorism expert:

> The fundamental nature and character of terrorism changed with 9/11 and moreover has continued to change and evolve since then. It is becoming increasingly difficult to categorize or pigeonhole as identifiable phenomena, amenable to categorization or clear distinction. The traditional way of understanding terrorism and looking at terrorists based on organizational definitions and attributes in some cases is no longer relevant. Increasingly, lone individuals with no connection with or formal ties to established or identifiable terrorist organizations are rising up to engage in violence. These individuals are often inspired or motivated by some larger political movement that they are not a part of, but nonetheless draw spiritual and emotional sustenance. Indeed, over the past 10 years or so—with the exception of the two World Trade Center attacks and that on the Pentagon—all of the most significant terrorist incidents that occurred in the United States were perpetrated either by a lone individual or very tight two- or three-man conspiratorial cells.

---

[1] K. J. Riley and B. Hoffman, *Domestic Terrorism: A National Assessment of State and Local Preparedness*, Santa Monica, Calif.: RAND Corporation, MR-505-NIJ, 1995.

> . . . the metric of success in the war on terrorism is defined as the ability of intelligence agencies and law enforcement organizations to prevent, preempt, and deter attacks.[2]

The growing threat of terrorism confronting the United States has required renewed attention by the law enforcement community. In addition to the prevention and deterrence of terrorist attacks, law enforcement plays a critical role in responding to and ensuring state and local preparedness for terrorism-related incidents. Such incidents (particularly those involving the use of chemical, biological, radiological, or nuclear [CBRN] weapons) require that law enforcement be able to operate in hazardous environments that police, unlike fire departments, for the most part have not confronted before. LaTourrette et al.'s study of emergency responder protection needs conducted after the 9/11 attacks found that a common concern expressed by law enforcement interviewees was the need for adequate protection against terrorist attacks involving the use of CBRN and the vulnerability of nonspecialist responders.[3]

In addition, law enforcement's overall mission is arguably broader than that of other first responders (e.g., fire service), encompassing a wider range of public safety responsibilities, of which preventing, deterring, and responding to terrorist threats is one among many. Gathering and sharing intelligence information on the terrorist threat facing one's jurisdiction or state requires new capabilities and the removal of institutional and structural barriers to interagency coordination in order to inform federal, state, and local counterterrorism and emergency preparedness efforts today.

Preparedness is comprised of a number of elements that any model of U.S. domestic preparedness for terrorism must take into account, including

---

[2] B. Hoffman, *Al Qaeda, Trends in Terrorism and Future Potentialities: An Assessment,* Santa Monica, Calif.: RAND Corporation, P-8078, 2003, pp. 16–17.

[3] T. LaTourrette, D. J. Peterson, J. T. Bartis, and B. A. Jackson, *Protecting Emergency Responders,* Vol. 2: *Community Views of Safety and Health Risks and Personal Protection Needs,* Santa Monica, Calif.: RAND Corporation, MR-1646-NIOSH, 2003.

- assessment activities (of the threat, of one's jurisdiction's or region's vulnerabilities, and of support needs)
- planning activities (e.g., development of contingency plans, updating of mutual aid agreements or response plans)
- training activities (e.g., field or tabletop exercises, counterterrorism training, courses related to weapons of mass destruction [WMD])
- equipping activities (e.g., purchase of personal protective equipment [PPE] and training of personnel on its use)
- coordination activities (for planning and training, intelligence gathering and information sharing, investigations, and communications during an emergency)
- organizational structures (e.g., specialized terrorism units) to improve one's response capabilities and investigative and intelligence capacities
- resourcing activities.

Our 2002 survey was able to collect information on many of these elements.

In this chapter, we examine what preparedness activities state and local law enforcement agencies have undertaken to counter the threat of terrorism and to shore up vulnerabilities. The results are presented in six areas: (1) assessment activities before and after 9/11; (2) coordination activities on intelligence and with interagency task forces; (3) communications capabilities, including interoperability challenges; (4) organizational changes made to improve response capabilities; (5) planning activities; and (6) training activities, including participation in federal preparedness programs. We begin with a brief discussion of our analytic approach and conclude with a discussion summarizing the key findings within the chapter.

Analytic Approach

Using the survey data, we conducted descriptive analyses presenting the weighted results to represent the national estimate of local law enforcement agencies—an estimate that accounts for our sample design and for nonresponse bias. For state law enforcement organizations, no weighting was necessary since we undertook a census of these organizations. As noted in Chapter One, we used a finite population correction to derive the standard errors for these state-level organizations. (See the discussions in Chapter One and Appendix A.)

In addition, we assessed differences between law enforcement agencies by county size. We present the results for local law enforcement overall and then broken down by those law enforcement agencies located in large metropolitan ("metro") counties (i.e., central counties of metropolitan areas with a population of 1 million or more)[4] and by those agencies located in smaller ("non-metro") counties (i.e., counties with a population of less than 1 million).

Assessment Activities Before and After 9/11

Even before 9/11, state and local responders had conducted various types of assessments as part of the requirements of different federal preparedness programs. In 2000, under the auspices of the Office of Justice Programs' (OJP) Office of State and Local Domestic Preparedness Support (OSLDPS) and as part of the State Domestic Preparedness Equipment Program, state and local governments were required to conduct a needs assessment. Each jurisdiction was to assess its requirements for equipment, training, and other resources related to response to incidents involving the use of WMD and terrorist incidents involving the use of chemical or biological agents, radiological explosives, and incendiary devices. In addition, each state was to develop a Two-Year Statewide Domestic Preparedness Strategy that would be used as a guide to target grant funds received and to provide OJP guidance on how best to target first responder training and other resources available through its program.[5]

---

[4] Definition is based on Office of Research and Planning, Bureau of Health Professions, Area Resource File, 2000.

[5] Office for State and Local Domestic Preparedness Support, *Fiscal Year 2000 State Domestic Preparedness Equipment Program*, http://www.ojp.usdoj.gov/fundopps.htm.

When the Nunn-Lugar-Domenici (NLD) Domestic Preparedness Program (DPP) was transferred to DOJ's OSLDPS in October 2000, program participants were asked in the second round of the NLD DPP to complete threat and vulnerability assessments in conjunction with receipt of resources and to participate in the statewide assessment process associated with the OSLDPS State Domestic Preparedness Equipment Program.[6]

The initial assessments, conducted in 2000–2001, were to be updated in fall 2003 as part of ODP's State Homeland Security Assessment and Strategy (SHSAS) process.[7] In 2003, ODP directed states to conduct threat and vulnerability assessments, as well as assessments of capabilities and needs, to serve as inputs into the statewide Homeland Security Strategy.[8] Program participants in the State Homeland Security Grant Program (SHSGP) and the Urban Area Security Initiative (UASI) were required to conduct threat, vulnerability, and needs assessments using a structured chemical, biological, radiological, nuclear, or explosives (CBRNE) assessment tool developed by ODP.[9] The results of these assessments were to be used in developing a Homeland Security Strategy to serve as the basis for targeting preparedness-improvement efforts and for the allocation of grant funds.

RAND's survey was conducted in fall 2002, after the initial 2001 statewide assessment process and a year before the 2003 updating of

---

[6] OSLDPS, *Fiscal Year 2001, Nunn-Lugar-Domenici Domestic Preparedness Program: Program Guidelines and Kit*, Washington, D.C.: U.S. Department of Justice, Office of Justice Programs, Office for State and Local Domestic Preparedness Support, 2001.

[7] In 2001, OSLDPS was renamed ODP. ODP administered the 2001 State Domestic Preparedness Equipment Program that provided direct grants to states and local jurisdictions for planning, training, equipment, and exercises. Many of the initial orders by law enforcement agencies for PPE occurred during this process. In spring 2003, ODP was transferred to the new DHS.

[8] DHS, Office of the Press Secretary, "Secretary of Homeland Security Tom Ridge Visited the National Emergency Training Center," Washington, D.C., June 26, 2003. Online at http://www.dhs.gov/dhspublic/interapp/press_release/press_release_0195.xml (as of February 2, 2004).

[9] ODP administers two major grant programs whose aim is to enhance state and local preparedness: (a) SHSGP, a formula grant program to fund equipment, exercises, training, planning, and critical infrastructure protection; and (b) UASI, which provides grant funds to meet the equipment, training, planning, and exercise needs of large urban areas. Initial participants in the UASI program include 30 large urban areas, 14 major ports, 20 mass transit systems, and 2 radiological defense systems.

those statewide assessments. We asked state and local law enforcement agencies specifically about their assessment activities both in the year prior to and the year following the 9/11 attacks. We did not ask them if their assessment activities were undertaken as part of a specific grant program or were done on their own initiative.

Most state and local law enforcement agencies conducted a risk or threat assessment between 2000 and 2002 (Table 3.1). Prior to 9/11, state law enforcement agencies were more proactive than local law enforcement in doing assessments: whereas 44 percent of state law enforcement agencies had conducted an assessment prior to 9/11, only 30 percent of local law enforcement agencies had done so. Following 9/11, an equal percentage of state agencies also conducted an assessment as had done so previously. In addition, 9 percent of state law enforcement agencies indicated they had done an assessment both prior to and following 9/11. For state law enforcement, responsibility for conducting the assessment(s) fell for the most part upon their department or an interagency task force (Table 3.1).[10]

The 9/11 terrorist attacks, along with ODP's domestic preparedness programs, appear to have made a difference in increasing assessment activities at the local level. Of local law enforcement agencies that conducted an assessment during the two-year period, about two-thirds did so following 9/11 (Table 3.1). These assessment activities at the local level do not appear to be strongly associated with the NLD program. Although the second round of the NLD program required participants to do an assessment, only 5 percent of local agencies in our sample reported participation in that program.[11] Since the second round of the SHSAS did not begin until 2003, this increase in assessment activities following 9/11 cannot be attributed to the second wave of statewide assessments.

---

[10] The "Other" category in Table 3.1 includes private security firms, other city departments such as Public Works, offices of emergency services, U.S. Marshals, and special task forces or response teams.

[11] It is possible that participation in the NLD program may be underreported in our survey, depending on how knowledgeable the individual filling out the survey instrument was of their department's participation since 1996 in different federal programs. Regardless, the result suggests that only a small fraction of local departments in our sample were participants in the NLD program.

Table 3.1
Between 2000–2002, Did Law Enforcement Agencies Conduct Risk or Threat Assessments?

Conducted an Assessment?	All State LE Orgs. (%)	All Local LE Orgs. (%)
Yes	82 (3)	73 (8)
If So, When Was It Conducted?	**State LE Orgs. That Conducted an Assessment (%)**	**Local LE Orgs. That Conducted an Assessment (%)**
During the year before 9/11	44 (5)	30 (11)
During the year after 9/11	41 (5)	68 (11)
Who Conducted the Assessment?	**State LE Orgs. That Conducted an Assessment (%)**	**Local LE Orgs. That Conducted an Assessment (%)**
Their Department	59 (6)	62 (12)
Interagency task force	44 (6)	42 (13)
Another org. within jurisdiction	15 (4)	9 (5)
FBI	11 (4)	2 (2)
Other federal agency/dept. (e.g., FDA, EPA)	11 (4)	2 (2)
Other	22 (5)	14 (7)

Standard error of the estimate shown in parentheses. Respondents were asked to mark all that apply on the question about who conducted the assessment.

Overall, the assessments undertaken at the state level tended to be broader in scope than those at the local level. Most state agencies' assessment activities focused on key infrastructure, public buildings, government or military facilities, and their own departments (Table 3.2). Assessments done at the local level primarily focused on public buildings and key infrastructure.

To better understand differences in assessment strategies at the local level, we compared law enforcement agencies in large metropolitan counties with those in smaller counties. Law enforcement agencies in large counties were similar to state law enforcement agencies in being proactive before 9/11 in doing assessments (Tables 3.1 and 3.3). However, following the 9/11 attacks, agencies in smaller counties worked to catch up. Whereas only 25 percent of them had conducted an assessment before 9/11, approximately 75 percent of law enforcement agencies in smaller counties did so in the year following the terrorist attacks (Table

Table 3.2
Of those Law Enforcement Agencies That Conducted an Assessment, What Was Its Focus?

Assessment Focus	State LE Orgs. That Conducted an Assessment (%)	Local LE Orgs. That Conducted an Assessment (%)
Key public buildings	85 (4)	89 (6)
Key infrastructure (power, water, electricity, etc.)	93 (3)	73 (19)
Own department	81 (5)	51 (15)
Government or military facilities	85 (4)	37 (12)
Chemical plants	63 (6)	26 (11)
Agricultural facilities	44 (6)	17 (8)
Food processing/packing plants	37 (6)	13 (7)
Other private businesses	37 (6)	27 (10)
Other	22 (5)	19 (9)

Standard error of the estimate shown in parentheses. Respondents were asked to check all that apply.

3.3). For the majority of local law enforcement agencies, responsibility for conducting an assessment fell upon either their department or an interagency task force (Table 3.3). Agencies in large counties were somewhat more likely to have their department responsible for doing these assessments; whereas smaller counties appeared to rely more on interagency task forces. The focus of the assessments also varied by size of jurisdiction. Assessments done by law enforcement agencies in large counties tended to be broader in scope (similar to that of state agencies) than those done by agencies in smaller counties (Table 3.3).

These results suggest variation, particularly at the local level, in assessment strategies and, as discussed in the next chapter, possible differences by size of jurisdiction in law enforcement's support needs for doing future assessments.

Coordination Activities

Coordination on Intelligence Sharing and Investigations

Since 9/11, a major concern of the law enforcement community has been the need to improve coordination between the federal, state, and

Table 3.3
Assessment Activites of Local Law Enforcement Agencies, by Size of Jurisdiction

	Of Those Local LE Orgs. That Conducted an Assessment (%)		
When Was the Assessment Conducted?	**Overall**	**Metro**	**Non-Metro**
Before 9/11	30 (11)	46 (16)	25 (12)
After 9/11	68 (11)	43 (14)	75 (12)
Who Conducted the Assessment?	**Overall**	**Metro**	**Non-Metro**
Their department	62 (12)	73 (11)	60 (16)
Interagency task force	42 (13)	19 (1)	47 (17)
Another org. within jurisdiction	9 (5)	3 (2)	11 (7)
What was the Assessment's Focus?	**Overall**	**Metro**	**Non-Metro**
Key public buildings	89 (6)	96 (2)	88 (7)
Key infrastructure	73 (19)	91 (5)	68 (22)
Own department	51 (15)	86 (7)	43 (16)
Government or military facilities	37 (12)	65 (14)	30 (12)
Chemical plants	26 (11)	42 (19)	23 (11)
Agricultural facilities	17 (8)	36 (20)	12 (7)
Food Processing/packing plants	13 (7)	35 (20)	8 (5)
Other private businesses	27 (10)	59 (14)	19 (9)
Other	19 (9)	7 (4)	22 (11)

Standard error of the estimate shown in parentheses. Respondents were asked to mark all that apply on the question about who conducted the assessment.

local levels on the gathering and sharing of intelligence information and on terrorist investigations. The U.S. Attorney General has designated the FBI to be the lead federal law enforcement agency for investigating acts of domestic and international terrorism. Prior to 9/11, the FBI established Joint Terrorism Task Forces (JTTFs)[12] in their field

---

[12] The first JTTF was established in New York City in 1980. The JTTFs vary in size and structure in relation to the terrorist threat dealt with by each FBI field office. On average, 40 to 50 people are assigned full-time to the JTTFs; however, some task forces, such as the one in New York City, can have as many as 500 personnel and a number of part-time personnel. DOJ, Office of the Inspector General, *The Federal Bureau of Investigation's Efforts to Improve the Sharing of Intelligence and Other Information,* Audit Report No. 04-10, December 2003.

offices, comprised of teams of state and local law enforcement agencies, FBI agents, and representatives of other federal agencies.[13] These task forces (along with FBI field offices) were to be responsible for investigations involving international and domestic acts of terrorism and the use of WMD and for national infrastructure protection.[14] As part of the FBI's efforts to improve information sharing and coordination between federal, state, and local law enforcement agencies, the FBI increased the number of JTTFs from 36 in 2001 to 84 in 2003.[15] Depending on the nature of the threat, other federal agencies (e.g., the Secret Service, Immigration and Naturalization Service [INS], Federal Aviation Administration [FAA], or Drug Enforcement Administration [DEA]) may also get involved in terrorist-related investigations.

We were interested in understanding the degree to which state and local law enforcement agencies are coordinating with the FBI and with other federal agencies. Specifically, how many law enforcement agencies received guidance from the FBI following 9/11 as to what type of information about the terrorist threat they should collect and pass on? To what extent have state and local law enforcement coordinated with the FBI's counterterrorism personnel during the past five years, and in what ways? What other federal agencies have state and local law enforcement coordinated with on terrorist-related investigations?

Following 9/11, most state and local law enforcement agencies had received guidance from the FBI as to what type of information about suspected terrorist activities they should collect and pass on to the Bureau (Table 3.4). While 95 percent of state law enforcement agencies had coordinated in some capacity with the FBI's JTTFs during the past five years, only about a third of local law enforcement agencies had done so (Table 3.5). Among state law enforcement agencies, the primary reasons for interacting with the JTTFs were to provide assistance with an investigation or to share intelligence on the terrorist threat within their state. Few local law enforcement agencies reported having assisted the

---

[13] FBI, War on Terrorism: Counterterrorism, http://www.fbi.gov/terrorinfo/counterrorism/partnership.htm (as of December 9, 2003).

[14] DOJ, Office of the Inspector General, December 2003, p. 42.

[15] DOJ, Office of the Inspector General, December 2003, p. 42.

Table 3.4
Received Guidance from the FBI Following 9/11

	State Law Enforcement	Local Law Enforcement		
		All Local LE Orgs. (%)		
Receive Guidance from the FBI Following 9/11 as to What Information to Collect and Pass On?	All State LE Orgs. (%)	Overall	Metro	Non-Metro
Yes, received guidance	72 (7)	57 (12)	92 (3)	49 (14)

Standard error of the estimate shown in parentheses. The purposes for which agencies have interacted with the FBI's JTTFs represent a lower-bound estimate for each category. Respondents were asked to check only one answer. Of the 112 local law enforcement agencies that answered this question, 83 followed instructions and checked one category only; 29 checked multiple categories. Of the 37 state law enforcement agencies that answered this question, 23 followed instructions and checked one category only; 14 checked multiple categories. For each group, we report here the combined results.

JTTFs with an investigation.[16] Instead, the primary reasons for local law enforcement to interact with the JTTFs were to share intelligence information or to receive counterterrorism training. In comparison, relatively few state law enforcement agencies reported receiving counterterrorism training from the JTTFs, suggesting that these state-level organizations were obtaining such training from other sources.[17]

There were also some key differences by size of jurisdiction. Following 9/11, almost all law enforcement agencies in large counties received guidance from the FBI as to what type of information they should collect and pass on about the terrorist threat, as compared to only half of law enforcement agencies in smaller counties (Table 3.4). Similar to state law enforcement agencies, the majority of law enforcement agen-

[16] The low level of involvement of local law enforcement agencies in investigations is not surprising given that the FBI has authority over, and responsibility for, investigation of all terrorist incidents in the United States, and given that the FBI would assume jurisdiction over a case if a local investigation revealed a terrorism connection. Riley and Hoffman, 1995.

[17] A number of federal agencies and private and nonprofit organizations provide counterterrorism training. This has led to DOJ creating the Counter-Terrorism Training and Resources for Law Enforcement Web site, which is intended to serve as a single point of access on counterterrorism training opportunities and related materials. See http://www.counterterrorismtraining.gov/mission/index.html (accessed April 30, 2004).

Table 3.5
Coordination with FBI's Joint Terrorism Task Forces (JTTFs)

	State Law Enforcement	Local Law Enforcement		
		All Local LE Orgs. (%)		
Coordinated with the FBI's JTTFs?	**All State LE Orgs. (%)**	**Overall**	**Metro**	**Non-Metro**
Yes, coordinated	92 (2)	36 (9)	88 (5)	24 (9)
Of Those Agencies That Had Coordinated With the JTTFs, For What Primary Purpose?		Local LE Orgs. (%)		
Purpose	**State LE Orgs. (%)**	**Overall**	**Metro**	**Non-Metro**
Assist with an investigation	68 (4)	17 (6)	17 (7)	18 (9)
Share intelligence information	41 (4)	64 (11)	40 (13)	84 (8)
Receive counterterrorism training	24 (4)	44 (11)	62 (13)	29 (15)
Other purposes	24 (4)	6 (3)	3 (1)	8 (5)

Standard error of the estimate shown in parentheses. The purposes for which agencies have interacted with the FBI's JTTFs represent a lower-bound estimate for each category. Respondents were asked to check only one answer. Of the 112 local law enforcement agencies that answered this question, 83 followed instructions and checked one category only; 29 checked multiple categories. Of the 37 state law enforcement agencies that answered this question, 23 followed instructions and checked one category only; 14 checked multiple categories. For each group, we report here the combined results.

cies in large counties had coordinated with the JTTFs within the past five years (as compared to only a quarter of law enforcement agencies in smaller counties) (Table 3.5). Of those law enforcement agencies in the large counties that had coordinated with the JTTFs, about two-thirds of them had done so to receive counterterrorism training (Table 3.5). In contrast, law enforcement agencies in smaller counties had interacted with the JTTFs primarily to share intelligence information.

What other federal agencies have state and local law enforcement agencies coordinated with on terrorist-related investigations during the past five years? In addition to assisting the FBI, a number of state law enforcement agencies also have coordinated with the INS, ATF, and DEA (Table 3.6).

Table 3.6
Coordination on Terrorist Investigation(s) with other Federal Agencies[a] During the Past 5 Years

Of Those That Had Coordinated with Other Fed. Agencies				
		Local LE Orgs. (%)		
With Which Agencies?	State LE Orgs. (%)	Overall	Metro	Non-Metro
DOE	31 (5)	5 (3)	10 (8)	0
FAA	50 (5)	55 (15)	56 (24)	55 (19)
Department of State	16 (4)	6 (3)	8 (5)	4 (4)
Secret Service	53 (5)	21 (9)	22 (14)	20 (12)
ATF	81 (4)	44 (15)	25 (14)	60 (20)
Customs Service	63 (5)	11 (6)	11 (7)	12 (9)
INS	81 (4)	28 (13)	13 (8)	41 (20)
DEA	72 (5)	27 (11)	18 (13)	34 (17)
Other	16 (4)	14 (8)	3 (2)	22 (14)

Standard error of the estimate shown in parentheses.

[a]That is, federal agencies other than the FBI. Respondents were asked to mark all that apply in identifying which agencies they had coordinated with in the past five years on terrorist-related investigations.

In comparison, most local law enforcement agencies (80 percent, S.E. 7) had not coordinated with other federal agencies (i.e., other than the FBI) on terrorist-related investigations (not shown). Of those that had, law enforcement in large counties was more likely than law enforcement in smaller counties to have done so (45 percent versus 14 percent) (not shown). The federal agencies with which local law enforcement had coordinated during the past five years have primarily been the FAA and the ATF. Law enforcement in smaller counties had coordinated also with the INS and the DEA on investigations.

Coordination with Interagency Task Forces to Improve Response Capabilities

Planning, emergency response, and preparedness are not solely the responsibility of individual departments, but that of many agencies and organizations, underscoring the importance of coordination between first responders and other key players. A number of interagency task forces have been established at the federal, state, and local levels to improve coordination on emergency preparedness and response, both in general and for terrorism specifically. We asked about law enforcement agencies' participation in various terrorism-related task forces, many of which had been established (or had their mission expanded) following the 9/11 attacks.

In general, state law enforcement agencies had greater participation in terrorist-related task forces than had local law enforcement. Nearly all state law enforcement agencies either formally liased with or were official members of at least one terrorism-related task force (Table 3.7). At the federal level, they liaised with primarily the JTTFs, and at the state level, with their state attorney general's Anti-Terrorism Task Forces (ATTFs) or their state's Homeland Security Office task force. One out of five state law enforcement agencies also liaised with city and county interagency task forces. Most state law enforcement agencies reported having formal protocols for coordinating with these task forces in the event of a terrorist-related incident (not shown).

In comparison, less than half of local law enforcement agencies either formally liased with or were an official member of at least one terrorism-related task force (Table 3.7). Other than the FBI's JTTFs, the primary task forces local law enforcement liaised with were city and county interagency task forces or their state attorney general's ATTF.[18] Of those local law enforcement agencies that did coordinate with at least one terrorism-related task force, most (80 percent, S.E. 9) reported having formal protocols for doing so in the event of a terrorist-related incident (not shown).

Communications Interoperability

The recent 9/11 Commission hearings highlighted what communications problems emergency responders encountered in responding to the 9/11 attacks, with lack of interoperability being one of the key factors. For example, the orders to evacuate the entire World Trade Center complex issued within ten minutes of American Airlines Flight 11 hitting the

---

[18] There were no significant differences between law enforcement agencies in large versus small counties in the types of task forces that they participated in.

Table 3.7
Which Terrorism-related Task Forces Do Law Enforcement Agencies Belong to or Formally Liaise With?

Liaise with or Member of?	All State LE Orgs. (%)	All Local LE Orgs. (%)
Yes	90 (2)	42 (11)
Of Those That Do, with Which Task Force(s)?	**State LE Orgs. That Liaised with or Were a Member (%)**	**Local LE Orgs. That Liaised with or Were a Member (%)**
FBI's JTTFs	89 (3)	36 (9)
State Attorney General's ATTF	77 (4)	44 (11)
State Homeland Security Office task force	77 (4)	23 (8)
City/county task forces	20 (4)	42 (10)
Other task force(s)	17 (4)	10 (10)

Standard error of the estimate shown in parentheses.

north tower could be heard only by officers listening to the command channel of the Port Authority of New York and the New Jersey police. It was unclear whether this order had been communicated to officers in other Port Authority police commands or to emergency personnel of other responding agencies. In addition, because the city's fire department radios had not yet been upgraded to a digital system, firefighters were unable to communicate with other agencies' radio systems.[19]

In our 2002 survey, we asked law enforcement agencies to rate their department's ability to communicate with other emergency response organizations in the event of a large-scale emergency involving multiple agencies or jurisdictions, using a scale from 1 to 5 where 1 = inadequate and 5 = excellent. We defined interoperability as the ability of law enforcement personnel to communicate in real time with other response personnel from multiple agencies and/or jurisdictions via radio or telephone in order to mount a well-coordinated response.

One year following the 9/11 attacks, state law enforcement agencies and local law enforcement agencies in large counties rated their de-

[19] P. Hirschkorn, "9/11 Panel Focuses on Rescue Efforts: Communication Troubles Cited in Response to New York Attacks," CNN, May 18, 2004, http://www.cnn.com/2004/US/05/18/911.commission/ (accessed June 4, 2004).

partment's ability to communicate with other responding organizations as barely adequate, with law enforcement agencies in smaller counties assigning a somewhat higher rating to their department (Table 3.8). These differences in ratings of departments' communications abilities may reflect in part the fact that law enforcement agencies in smaller counties tend to have fewer organizations to coordinate and so may find it easier to find workarounds to interoperability problems; state agencies and law enforcement in larger counties tend to have more experience with multiagency response and so more opportunities to identify interoperability problems.

Improving communications interoperability was a priority for most state and local law enforcement agencies (Table 3.8). All state law enforcement agencies and about three-quarters of local law enforcement agencies cited interoperability shortfalls (Table 3.8). The three major factors cited as limiting interoperability were lack of funding, aging communications systems and hardware, and frequency incompatibility between response organizations. Aging communications systems and hardware was a particularly important limiting factor for state law enforcement agencies (74 percent) and for law enforcement agencies in smaller counties (47 percent). Frequency incompatibility was an important limiting factor for a majority of state law enforcement (71 percent) and local law enforcement agencies in large counties (56 percent). Differences in resource priorities between emergency response organizations were also cited by 26 percent of state law enforcement agencies and 15 percent of law enforcement agencies in large counties as hindering efforts to improve interoperability within their jurisdiction or region. Factors limiting interoperability also are interrelated. For example, lack of funding contributes to an inability to update aging communications systems and possibly to differences between emergency responder agencies in their resource priorities.

Organizational Changes Made to Improve Terrorism Response Capabilities

What organizational changes did law enforcement make to improve their capabilities to address terrorism? Following 9/11, nearly half of state law enforcement agencies, but few local law enforcement agen-

Table 3.8
Adequacy of Interagency Communications and Factors That Limit Interoperability

	State Law Enforcement	Local Law Enforcement		
		Mean Rating of Local LE Orgs.		
Rating of Dept.'s Ability to communicate with Other Orgs. Involved in a Multiagency Response	**Mean Rating of State LE Orgs.**	**Overall**	**Metro**	**Non-Metro**
Rating of Communications Adequacy (scale of 1 to 5; 1=Inadequate, 5=Excellent)	3.0 (0.2)	3.4 (0.3)	2.9 (0.5)	3.5 (0.4)
		Local LE Orgs. (%)		
Any Limitations to Interoperability?	**All State LE Orgs. (%)**	**Overall**	**Metro**	**Non-Metro**
Yes	100 (0)	74 (15)	84 (9)	71 (18)
		Local LE Orgs. with Limits (%)		
If Yes, What Factors Limit Interoper-Ability of Dept.'s Comm. System?	**State LE Orgs. with Limits (%)**	**Overall**	**Metro**	**Non-Metro**
Aging communications system and hardware	74 (7)	43 (11)	27 (9)	47 (14)
Lack of information or guidance on what technologies to buy	5 (4)	8 (4)	12 (6)	7 (5)
Uncertainty surrounding the availability of spectrum for public safety use	11 (5)	0.7 (0.4)	3 (2)	0.1 (0.1)
Frequency incompatibility between emergency response orgs.	71 (7)	43 (11)	56 (13)	40 (13)
Lack of funding	79 (7)	56 (13)	39 (11)	61 (16)
Not a priority for our department	0	3 (2)	2 (2)	4 (3)
Differences in rules and regulations between jurisdictions	3 (3)	5 (3)	10 (5)	4 (3)
Differences in resource priorities between response orgs.	26 (7)	8 (3)	15 (7)	6 (4)

Standard error of the estimate shown in parentheses.

cies, increased the number of personnel assigned (full time or part time) to do emergency response planning for terrorist-related incidents (Table 3.9). Following 9/11, law enforcement agencies in large counties were about three times more likely to have increased the number of personnel doing response planning than agencies located in smaller counties (Table 3.9).

Law enforcement agencies were asked if they had specialized units, sections, groups, or individuals specifically assigned responsibility for addressing terrorism for their department. In general, many more state law enforcement agencies (77 percent) reported having such a specialized terrorism unit than did local law enforcement agencies (16 percent) (Table 3.10). In addition, 64 percent (S.E. 8) of state law enforcement agencies reported having a separate criminal intelligence unit, as compared to only 10 percent of local law enforcement agencies (not shown). At the local level, more commonly, law enforcement agencies (49 percent) had narcotics units with other types of specialized units listed, including gang abatement, organized crime, white-collar crime, and hate crimes (not shown).[20]

At the state and local levels, most of the specialized terrorism units were responsible for liaising with other law enforcement agen-

Table 3.9
Following 9/11, Did Law Enforcement Increase Number of Personnel Assigned to Do Emergency Response Planning for Terrorist-related Incidents?

	State Law Enforcement	Local Law Enforcement		
		All Local LE Orgs. (%)		
Increase Number of Personnel Assigned (Full-time or Part-time) to Do Response Planning for Terrorist-related Incidents?	All State LE Orgs. (%)	Overall	Metro	Non-Metro
Yes	46 (6)	6 (3)	14 (5)	4 (3)

Standard error of the estimate shown in parentheses.

[20] Overall, 49 percent of agencies had narcotics units, 10 percent had general criminal-intelligence units, 9 percent had gang-abatement units, 8 percent had white-collar-crime units, 6 percent had hate-crime units, 4 percent had organized-crime units, and 17 percent had other types of units (e.g., SWAT, bomb squads, domestic-violence units, drug task forces, or computer-crime units).

Table 3.10
Percentage of Law Enforcement with Specialized Terrorism Units

	State Law Enforcement	Local Law Enforcement		
		All Local LE Orgs. (%)		
Specialized Unit/ Section/ Group?	**All State LE Orgs. (%)**	**Overall**	**Metro**	**Non-Metro**
Yes	77 (3)	16 (5)	26 (8)	14 (6)
		Local LE Orgs. with Specialized Unit (%)		
What Are Its Duties?	**State LE Orgs. with Specialized Unit (%)**	**Overall**	**Metro**	**Non-Metro**
Liaise with other law enforcement agencies	90 (4)	97 (2)	93 (4)	100
Intelligence gathering	83 (4)	88 (5)	72 (10)	94 (5)
Analyze and disseminate information	87 (4)	60 (13)	70 (11)	56 (19)
Liaise with federal agencies	90 (4)	51 (13)	67 (12)	44 (17)
Provide intelligence information to other law enforcement agencies	87 (4)	50 (13)	55 (12)	48 (18)
Training of other law enforcement personnel or agencies	57 (6)	38 (13)	23 (8)	45 (18)
Provide resources to other law enforcement agencies	50 (6)	28 (9)	29 (9)	27 (13)
Investigate specific terrorist incidents	67 (6)	15 (5)	23 (7)	11 (6)

Standard error of the estimate shown in parentheses.

cies and assisting with intelligence gathering. The responsibilities of these specialized units tended to be broader at the state level than at the local level. For example, whereas a third or fewer of local agencies' specialized units were involved in training other law enforcement personnel, investigation of incidents, or providing resources to other law enforcement agencies, these activities fell more into the purview of the specialized units of many state law enforcement agencies (Table 3.10). Similar to state law enforcement agencies, the specialized terrorism units of law enforcement agencies in large counties tended to have broader responsibilities, including analysis and dissemination of intelligence information, liaising with federal agencies, and assisting with investigations (Table 3.10).

Planning Activities

To what degree are law enforcement agencies responsible for developing emergency response and contingency plans for their jurisdiction to address terrorism-related incidents? Within large counties, responsibility for developing contingency plans for terrorist-related incidents tends to reside with local law enforcement (Table 3.11). However, in smaller counties, responsibility resides either with an interagency task force or with law enforcement. Somewhat unsettling was the result that 14 percent of local law enforcement agencies indicated that they did not know who was responsible for developing such contingency plans for their jurisdiction. Almost all local agencies (89 percent, S.E. 5) reported that these contingency plans were designed for multiagency use (not shown).

At the state level, responsibility for developing contingency plans tends to reside primarily with law enforcement (Table 3.11). Most state law enforcement agencies (95 percent, S.E. 2) indicated such contingency plans were designed for multiagency use (not shown).

With respect to mutual aid, most local law enforcement agencies (92 percent, S.E. 4) (not shown) have some form of mutual aid agreements with other city, county, regional, or state organizations for emergency response. However, relatively few local law enforcement agencies (about one out of ten) updated their existing mutual aid agreements or established new agreements in the year following 9/11 to specifically address emergency response for terrorist-related incidents (Table 3.12). This result could reflect less active engagement in updating mutual aid agreements at the local level, or perhaps many local law enforcement agencies feel that existing mutual aid agreements are sufficient to address their support needs for terrorist-related incidents as well.

In general, more law enforcement agencies in large counties established new mutual aid agreements following 9/11 for terrorist-related

Table 3.11
Are Law Enforcement Agencies Responsible for Developing Terrorism Contingency Response Plans for Their Jurisdiction or State?

	State Law Enforcement	Local Law Enforcement		
		All Local LE Orgs. (%)		
Responsible?	All State LE Orgs. (%)	Overall	Metro	Non-Metro
Yes, department is responsible	60 (4)	36 (9)	60 (12)	30 (10)
No, an interagency task force is	18 (3)	40 (12)	23 (9)	44 (15)
No, fire department is	3 (3)	5 (3)	3 (2)	6 (4)
No, another local/state agency Is	16 (6)	5 (3)	4 (2)	5 (4)
Don't know who Is responsible	3 (3)	14 (7)	10 (4)	15 (8)

Standard error of the estimate shown in parentheses.

incidents than did agencies in smaller counties (30 percent versus 7 percent) (Table 3.12). These results likely understate the amount of updating of mutual aid agreements done by law enforcement after 9/11, because we only asked about terrorist-related incidents; we did not ask if their departments had updated agreements for emergency response in general (i.e., consistent with an all-hazards approach to preparedness).

Although at the local level few agencies updated their mutual aid agreements following 9/11, local law enforcement appeared to be somewhat more proactive in updating their response plans or standard operating procedures (SOPs). One-third of law enforcement agencies in large counties and one-third of those in smaller counties updated their response plans primarily to address CBR-related incidents.[21]

Similar to local law enforcement, most state law enforcement agencies (85 percent, S.E. 3) already had some form of mutual aid agreements in place for emergency response in general (not shown). However, state law enforcement agencies were more actively engaged

[21] Although not shown, only 3 percent of local law enforcement agencies updated their response plans for agroterrorism-related incidents, and even fewer (less than 1 percent) had done so for cyberterrorism.

Table 3.12
Since 9/11, Have Law Enforcement Agencies Updated Their Mutual Aid Agreements or Response Plans Specifically to Address Terrorism-Related Incidents?

	State Law Enforcement	Local Law Enforcement		
		All Local LE Orgs. (%)		
Updated Mutual-Aid Agreements?	**All State LE Orgs. (%)**	**Overall**	**Metro**	**Non-Metro**
Updated existing mutual aid agreements	33 (5)	12 (5)	10 (4)	13 (6)
Established new mutual aid agreements	27 (5)	11 (6)	30 (16)	7 (5)
Updated Plans?		**Overall**	**Metro**	**Non-Metro**
Yes	69 (4)	27 (7)	33 (10)	25 (8)

Standard error of the estimate shown in parentheses.

in updating these agreements and their response plans. In response to 9/11, 69 percent of state law enforcement agencies updated their response plans or SOPs, as compared to only 27 percent of local law enforcement agencies. Also, about one-third of state law enforcement agencies updated their mutual aid agreements, and another third established new agreements to specifically address response to terrorist-related incidents (Table 3.12).

Training and Exercises

Law enforcement agencies can receive counterterrorism or antiterrorism training from a variety of sources, including ODP, the FBI, other federal agencies, private or nonprofit organizations, university programs, state government, or their police academy. We asked about law enforcement's training activities in several areas: (1) receipt of counterterrorism training from the FBI's JTTFs, and awareness of counterterrorism training being offered by their police academy or state government; (2) participation in interagency task forces in tabletop or field exercises; (3) participation of their department's specialized terrorism unit in joint training; and (4) participation in federally-sponsored training and equipment programs.

As noted earlier in this chapter, a number of local law enforcement agencies (particularly those in large counties) had received counterterrorism training from the FBI's JTTFs (see Table 3.5). However, relatively few state law enforcement agencies had received such training from the JTTFs, suggesting that these state-level organizations sought counterterrorism training from other sources.

Law enforcement agencies varied in their awareness of whether counterterrorism training was offered by their police academy or by the state. Whereas the JTTFs appear to be an oft-cited source of counterterrorism training at the local level, relatively few local law enforcement agencies (1 out of 20) reported that their police academy offered such training (Table 3.13). Law enforcement agencies in large counties were more likely to report that their police academy offered such training, as compared to agencies in smaller counties (17 percent versus 3 percent). Somewhat unsettling was the fact that about a third of local law enforcement agencies did not know whether their police academy offered this type of training.

We also asked whether their state offered counterterrorism or antiterrorism training (other than that offered by their police academy). The results were even more unsettling. Overall, 56 percent (S.E. 4) of

Table 3.13
Local Law Enforcement's Awareness of Counterterrorism or Antiterrorism Training Offered by Their Police Academy or State Government

	All Local LE Orgs. (%)		
Does Police Academy Offer Training?	**Overall**	**Metro**	**Non-Metro**
Yes	5 (2)	17 (8)	3 (2)
No	62 (10)	64 (11)	61 (12)
Don't know	33 (9)	20 (7)	36 (12)
Does State Offer Training?	**Overall**	**Metro**	**Non-Metro**
Yes	21 (7)	58 (12)	12 (5)
No	25 (8)	25 (9)	25 (10)
Don't know	53 (11)	17 (6)	62 (12)

Standard error of the estimate shown in parentheses.

state law enforcement agencies reported that their state offered counterterrorism or antiterrorism training (not shown). However, when we asked local law enforcement agencies, only 21 percent indicated awareness that their state offered such training (Table 3.13). Law enforcement agencies in smaller counties, in particular, were unaware of training offered by their state. Whereas 58 percent of law enforcement agencies in large counties reported that their state offered counterterrorism training, only 12 percent of agencies in smaller counties indicated this was the case. One might expect that law enforcement agencies in large counties are more likely to receive such training and, thus, might be more knowledgeable about training offered at the state level. In addition, the phrase *counterterrorism training* may have different meanings to different agencies. We did not attempt to define this term in the survey, and so some of the differences in reporting may be related to the different meanings attached to the term. However, the large discrepancy in knowledge at the local level about the training offered by their state suggests that this may be an area for improving awareness.

How proactive is law enforcement in conducting joint training on terrorism response, and with whom are they participating in such training? For the most part, local law enforcement agencies infrequently participated in joint training exercises with the interagency task force(s) of which they were members (Table 3.14). Of those local law enforcement agencies that participated in at least one terrorism-related task force, about two-thirds indicated that their department had never participated in exercises with these task forces (with the exception of city and county terrorism-related task forces). Participation in exercises was done either on an ad hoc basis or once a year. About a third of these law enforcement agencies had participated in tabletop or field exercises with their local city and county interagency task force on an ad hoc basis, and another third indicated that they did so once a year. This more active engagement at the local level in exercises suggests that city and county interagency task forces may be candidates for direct training dollars.

State law enforcement agencies also tended to participate on an ad hoc basis in field or tabletop exercises with the interagency task

Table 3.14
Frequency of Participation in Joint Exercises with Terrorism-Related Task Forces

	Of Those Local Agencies That Liaised with or Were Formal Members of Terrorist-related Task Forces, Frequency of Participation in Joint Exercises with other Orgs. (%)			
Task Forces	**Never**	**Once a Year**	**Twice a Year**	**Ad Hoc Basis**
FBI JTTFs	69 (10)	4 (3)	1 (1)	26 (10)
State attorney general ATTF	63 (13)	17 (12)	0	20 (10)
State homeland security office task force	60 (12)	19 (11)	1 (1)	21 (9)
City/county task force	34 (11)	29 (11)	6 (3)	31 (11)

Standard error of the estimate shown in parentheses.

forces they were members of. For example, about one-third of state law enforcement agencies reported participating in exercises on an ad hoc basis with the JTTFs and ATTFs; between 50 and 57 percent did so on an ad hoc basis with their state Homeland Security Office task force and with city and county task forces (not shown).

In general, law enforcement agencies with specialized terrorism units appear to be more proactive in doing joint training. Since 9/11, most state and local law enforcement agencies' specialized terrorism units had participated in joint training exercises (Table 3.15). At the local level, of the 16 percent of law enforcement agencies with specialized units, the majority reported that since 9/11 their units had participated in training exercises with other city or county agencies, and about a third had participated in joint training with state-level agencies or with the FBI (Table 3.15).

In general, state law enforcement's specialized terrorism units had conducted more joint training, with a greater variety of entities, than had the specialized units of local law enforcement. Of the 77 percent of state law enforcement agencies with specialized units, nearly all of these units (90 percent) had participated in joint training exercises since 9/11 (Table 3.15). About three-quarters of these specialized units had participated in joint training with other state agencies (in state) and about a third had done so with out-of-state agencies. In addition,

Table 3.15
Since 9/11, Has Specialized Unit/Section /Group/Individuals Participated in Any Joint Training Exercises?

	State Law Enforcement	Local Law Enforcement		
		Local LE Orgs. with Specialized Unit (%)		
Participated in Joint Training Exercises?	**State LE Orgs. with Specialized Unit (%)**	**Overall**	**Metro**	**Non-Metro**
Yes	90 (6)	79 (8)	60 (12)	87 (8)
		All Local LE Orgs. (%)		
If So, with Whom?	**All State LE Orgs. (%)**	**Overall**	**Metro**	**Non-Metro**
With other city or county agencies	43 (9)	66 (10)	46 (12)	75 (12)
With state agencies (in-state)	77 (8)	34 (12)	42 (11)	30 (18)
With state agencies (out-of-state)	33 (9)	6 (4)	14 (10)	2 (2)
With FBI	53 (9)	29 (10)	28 (9)	29 (14)
U.S. Secret Service	10 (6)	3 (2)	9 (6)	0
With DEA	10 (6)	6 (5)	2 (1)	8 (8)
With prof. associations, fraternal orgs. informal working groups	20 (7)	7 (3)	16 (7)	3 (3)

Standard error of the estimate shown in parentheses.

about half of these specialized units at the state level had done joint training with the FBI.[22]

Participation in Federally Sponsored Programs to Improve Domestic Preparedness for Terrorism

To understand to what degree law enforcement has participated in the different components of the U.S. domestic preparedness program, we asked survey respondents about their department's participation in federally sponsored training and equipment programs since 1996. Specifically, we gave survey respondents a list of training and equipment programs (shown in Table 3.16) and asked them to indicate those in which their

[22] Other entities that state agencies' specialized units conducted joint training with included the U.S. Secret Service (10 percent, standard error 6), the Border Patrol (13 percent, standard error 6), and DOE (10 percent, standard error 6) (not shown).

Table 3.16
Participation Since 1996 in Federally Sponsored Training and Equipment Programs

	State Law Enforcement	Local Law Enforcement
Participate in Any Federally Sponsored Training or Equipment Programs?	**All State LE Orgs. (%)**	**All Local LE Orgs. (%)**
Yes	83 (6)	25 (8)

Of Those Agencies That Had Participated In Federally Sponsored Training or Equipment Programs Since 1996...

Which Programs Did They Participate In?	State LE Orgs. That Participated (%)	Local LE Orgs. That Participated (%)
OJP First Responder Equipment Acquisition Program	50 (6)	14 (6)
Nunn-Lugar-Domenici Domestic Preparedness Program	40 (6)	12 (5)
OJP SLATT	37 (6)	23 (12)
OSLDPS training (DOJ-sponsored)	23 (5)	6 (4)
FEMA Emergency Management Institute Courses(s) (WMD-related)	60 (6)	38 (15)
U.S. Army Chemical School (USACLMS) training program	20 (5)	1 (1)
DOE training for radiological emergencies	23 (5)	3 (2)
New Mexico Tech's Incident Response to Terrorist Bombings Course	33 (6)	18 (12)
National Fire Academy Emergency Response to Terrorism Course(s)	30 (5)	4 (2)
FBI Hazardous Devices School	43 (6)	9 (5)
Other	23 (5)	24 (11)

Standard error of the estimate shown in parentheses.

department had participated. We also asked them to describe any other related training or equipment programs in which their department had participated but that had not been listed in the survey. The list given survey respondents was by no means exhaustive, given the vast number of training programs currently available. Also, it is possible that an individual filling out the survey may have been unaware of all of the programs or courses that their department had participated in since 1996. Therefore, these results should be interpreted cautiously, but are shown here to highlight general trends in program participation.

Most state law enforcement agencies (83 percent), but only a quarter of local law enforcement agencies, reported having participated in one or more federally sponsored programs for funding, equipment, or training since 1996 (Table 3.16). Eighty-three percent of state law enforcement agencies indicated that their department had participated in one or more of the programs listed in Table 3.16. In general, state law enforcement agencies have participated in a wider variety of antiterrorism and emergency preparedness programs (or courses) than has local law enforcement. Participation in the Federal Emergency Management Agency's (FEMA) Emergency Management Institute WMD-Related Courses(s), OJP's First Responder Equipment Acquisition Program, the NLD Domestic Preparedness Program, and OJP's State and Local Anti-Terrorism Training (SLATT) grant program were the most frequently cited programs by state law enforcement.

At the local level, only 25 percent of law enforcement agencies had participated in at least one of the programs listed in Table 3.16. For local law enforcement, FEMA's Emergency Management Institute WMD-Related Courses(s), OJP's SLATT grant program, and New Mexico Tech's Incident Response to Terrorist Bombings Courses were the most frequently cited programs or courses.

Discussion

9/11 Served as a Catalyst for Increasing Assessment Activities at the Local Level

Since the late 1990s, law enforcement agencies have conducted various types of assessments as part of the grant requirements of different federal preparedness programs. Of particular importance have been the statewide assessments undertaken in 2000–2001 and 2003 as part of the SHSAS process, the results of which were to serve as the basis for allocating grant funds and as input for targeting efforts to improve U.S. preparedness.

In general, the September 11 terrorist attacks, along with U.S. domestic preparedness programs, appear to have made a difference in terms of increasing assessment activities, particularly at the local level. Most state and local law enforcement agencies conducted a risk and/or threat assessment between 2000 and 2002. State law enforcement agencies and law enforcement agencies in large counties, in particular, were proactive in doing risk or threat assessments, even before the 9/11 attacks. Nearly 50 percent of these agencies had conducted an assessment before 9/11, and a similar percentage conducted assessments afterwards. Following 9/11, law enforcement agencies in smaller counties worked to catch up. Whereas only 25 percent of agencies in smaller counties had conducted an assessment before 9/11, approximately 75 percent of them did so following the 9/11 terrorist attacks.

Assessment activities at the state level and within large counties tended to be broader in scope and to be the responsibility primarily of law enforcement.[23] Within smaller counties, assessment activities tended to be narrower in scope (focusing mostly on public buildings and on key infrastructure), with many relying on interagency task forces (in addition to law enforcement) to conduct these assessments, suggesting that a somewhat different strategy was being employed within these counties.

In Response to 9/11, State and Local Law Enforcement Updated Response Plans and Less So Mutual-Aid Agreements

Following 9/11, approximately two-thirds of state law enforcement agencies and one-third of local law enforcement agencies (in both large and small counties) updated their response plans, primarily to address CBR-related incidents. About a third of state law enforcement agencies and local law enforcement agencies within large counties also updated their mutual aid agreements. However, few law enforcement agencies located within smaller counties updated mutual aid agreements, consistent with their lower threat perceptions. The relatively lower-level updating of mutual aid agreements in general is also consistent with an all-hazards approach to preparedness and perhaps with the belief that existing aid agreements were sufficient to meet law enforcement's support needs.

---

[23] Focusing on key infrastructure, public buildings, government or military facilities, and their own department's security.

At the state level and within large counties, responsibility for developing contingency plans for terrorist-related incidents tended to reside with law enforcement. In smaller counties, interagency task forces played a more important role in developing contingency plans (and in conducting assessments), suggesting that these counties have adopted a somewhat different strategy to addressing terrorism preparedness.

What other changes did law enforcement make to improve their planning capabilities? Following 9/11, nearly 50 percent of state law enforcement agencies, but only 6 percent of local law enforcement, increased the number of personnel they had assigned (full time or part time) to do emergency response planning for terrorist-related incidents.

Many Agencies Belong to Terrorist-Related Interagency Task Forces, but Infrequently Participate in Training Exercises with Them

Planning, emergency response, and preparedness are not solely the responsibility of individual departments, but that of many organizations, requiring effective coordination between first responders and other key players. A number of interagency task forces have been established at the federal, state, and local levels to improve coordination on emergency preparedness and response, in general and for terrorism, specifically with many having been established (or their mission expanded) after the 9/11 attacks.

Most state law enforcement agencies belonged to or formally liaised with at least one terrorism-related task force. The task forces that they primarily liaised with included the JTTFs, their state attorney general's ATTF, and their state's Homeland Security Office task force. In addition, one out of five state law enforcement agencies also liaised with local city and county interagency task forces. Although state law enforcement agencies participated in joint training exercises with a number of their associated task forces, most did so only an ad hoc basis or on an annual basis.

Fewer local law enforcement agencies were involved with such task forces. Less than half of local law enforcement agencies indicated they were a member of or formally liaised with a terrorism-related task force. Other than the FBI's JTTFs, the task forces with which local law enforcement primarily liased were city and county interagency task forces or their state's ATTF. For the most part, local law enforcement agencies infrequently participated in joint training exercises with these task forces, except for their local city or county task force. When they did so it was primarily on an ad hoc basis. The greater involvement of local law enforcement with city and county terrorism-related task forces, and the fact that one out of five state law enforcement agencies also liased with these task forces, suggests that these local entities may be possible candidates for training dollars.

Few Local Law Enforcement Agencies Have Specialized Terrorism Units

The majority of state law enforcement agencies had established a specialized terrorism unit or section, with two-thirds also having a separate criminal-intelligence unit. In comparison, relatively few local law enforcement agencies (16 percent) have a specialized terrorism unit, and only 10 percent have general criminal-intelligence units. Law enforcement agencies in large counties (26 percent) were somewhat more likely than those located in smaller counties to have established a specialized terrorism unit.

The primary responsibilities of these specialized terrorism units at the state and local levels were to liaise with other law enforcement agencies and assist with intelligence gathering. In addition, the responsibilities of terrorism units of state law enforcement agencies and local law enforcement within large counties also included training of other law enforcement personnel, assisting with investigations, and analysis and dissemination of intelligence information.

Law Enforcement Agencies with Specialized Terrorism Units Tended to Be More Actively Engaged in Training

How proactive was law enforcement in doing joint training on terrorism response, and with whom did they participate? Although most state and local law enforcement agencies infrequently participated in joint training exercises with their associated interagency task forces, it was a different story with respect to those agencies with specialized terrorism units.

Since 9/11, most of the specialized terrorism units established by state and local law enforcement agencies have participated in joint training exercises. At the local level, the majority of these units have done joint training with other city or county agencies or departments, and a third have participated in joint training with state-level agencies or the FBI. At the state level, three-quarters of these specialized terrorism units have participated in joint training exercises with other state agencies. In addition, about half of state law enforcement agencies' terrorism units had participated in joint training with the FBI.

For local law enforcement agencies, the FBI's JTTFs were an oft-cited source of counterterrorism training. This was not the case at the state level. Few state law enforcement agencies reported receiving counterterrorism training from the JTTFs, suggesting that these state-level organizations were obtaining such training from other sources. This result is not surprising given the proliferation of training courses available to law enforcement and the greater participation of state law enforcement agencies in federal preparedness programs.

State Law Enforcement Has Participated More in Federal Preparedness Programs than Has Local Law Enforcement

Starting in the mid-1990s, a series of terrorist incidents—for example, the 1993 New York World Trade Center bombing, the 1995 bombing of the Alfred P. Murrah Federal Building in Oklahoma City, and the March 1995 nerve gas attack in a Tokyo subway—helped spark the development of the U.S. domestic preparedness program.[24] These events heightened the awareness of emergency responders, security leaders, and policymakers of the critical need to improve U.S. response and deterrence capabilities. In 1996, the Defense Against Weapons of Mass Destruction Act (known as the Nunn-Lugar-Domenici amendment) directed the Secretary of Defense "to carry out a program to provide civilian personnel of federal, state, and local agencies with training and expert advice regarding emergency responses to a use or threatened use of a weapon of mass destruction or related materials."[25] Of the $100 million available

---

[24] R. A. Falkenrath, "The Problems of Preparedness: Challenges Facing the U.S. Domestic Preparedness Program," Cambridge, Mass.: John F. Kennedy School of Government, Harvard University, BCSIA Discussion Paper 2000-28, December 2000.

[25] Falkenrath, December 2000.

in FY 1997 for this purpose, approximately half of the funding went to the Department of Defense (DoD) to provide training to state and local responders, and the remainder was earmarked for other federal agencies or departments.[26] Since 1996, a variety of different federal programs and initiatives have been put into place to help improve state and local domestic preparedness for terrorism or incidents involving the use of CBRNE. By 2000, the U.S. domestic preparedness program had grown in size to more than $1 billion, with various initiatives having been established in different federal agencies.

State law enforcement agencies participated in more federal preparedness programs and in a wider variety of programs than has local law enforcement. In general, the majority (83 percent) of state law enforcement agencies reported that their department had participated in one or more federally sponsored training and equipping programs since 1996, as compared to only 25 percent of local law enforcement. Since 1996, about two-thirds of state law enforcement agencies and more than a third of local law enforcement agencies have attended the FEMA Emergency Management Institute's WMD-Related Courses. Fifty percent of state law enforcement agencies had also participated in OJP's First Responder Equipment Acquisition Program, and 37 percent in OJP's SLATT program. In comparison, only between 14 and 23 percent of local law enforcement agencies reported having participated in these two OJP programs.

However, the story is more complex than it appears on the surface. State law enforcement agencies likely used some of the federal support they received to help train local law enforcement and to assist with local planning activities. In other instances, state agencies may have served more as an administrator of federal preparedness grants and as a pass-through to local jurisdictions of federal support received. In addition, local law enforcement agencies' participation in federal preparedness programs may be understated. We asked survey respondents about their department's participation in federal programs since

---

[26] Falkenrath, December 2000. Of the $100 million made available in FY 1997, approximately half of it was provided to DoD to conduct training of state and local responders, and the remainder was earmarked for the Department of Health and Human Services (DHHS) ($6.5 million), DOJ ($17 million), FEMA ($15 million), and Customs ($9 million).

1996. It may be that some respondents were unaware of all the different programs or courses that their department had participated in during this five-year time period. In addition, other DOJ-related nonterrorism-specific programs have been an important source of funding for law enforcement. In addition to the SLATT program, the Community Oriented Police Services (COPS) Program and the Local Law Enforcement Block Grant Program have enabled law enforcement to hire additional personnel and to purchase equipment. In our survey, we only asked about participation in the SLATT program; we did not ask about the COPS program or other related programs.

State Law Enforcement Agencies and Those in Large Counties Have More Experience in Coordinating on Terrorism Investigations and Response

Most state and local law enforcement agencies (especially those in large counties) received guidance from the FBI following 9/11 as to the type of information about suspected terrorist activities they should collect and pass on. In general, state law enforcement agencies had more experience in coordinating with the FBI and other federal agencies on terrorist-related activities than had local law enforcement agencies. Between 1998 and 2002, 95 percent of state law enforcement agencies had coordinated in some capacity with the JTTFs, primarily to provide assistance with an investigation or to share intelligence information. In addition to the FBI, a number of state law enforcement agencies had coordinated on investigations with the INS, ATF, and DEA.

In comparison, between 1998 and 2002, only about a third of local law enforcement agencies had coordinated in some capacity with the FBI's JTTFs, primarily to share intelligence information or to receive counterterrorism training. We also found key differences in coordination activities by size of jurisdiction. Similar to state law enforcement agencies, the majority of law enforcement agencies in large counties had interactions with the JTTFs during this time period. They did so primarily to receive counterterrorism training or to share intelligence information. However, few law enforcement agencies in smaller counties had interacted with the JTTFs; when they had, it was primarily limited to sharing intelligence information. Further, few local law enforcement agencies had assisted the FBI's JTTFs or other federal agencies with a terrorist-related investigation during this five-year time period.

Variation in Response Experience and Approach to Preparedness by Size of County

Table 3.17 compares law enforcement agencies located within large counties (i.e., counties with a population of 1 million or more) with those within smaller counties in terms of their approach to preparedness, experience with terrorist-related incidents, and experience with coordinating on intelligence-related matters.

What is typical of the response experience of law enforcement agencies in large counties versus smaller counties, and in what ways do they differ? In response to 9/11 and the terrorist threat, law enforcement agencies within large counties were more proactive in addressing terrorism preparedness than those located in smaller counties. Consistent with their higher threat perceptions, law enforcement agencies in large counties were more likely to have

- increased the number of personnel assigned to do emergency response planning following 9/11
- specialized terrorism units, and to have those units participate in joint training
- conducted risk or threat assessments before 9/11
- more experience in responding to and assisting with terrorist-related investigations, and in coordinating with the FBI and other federal agencies.

However, they were similar in the updating of response plans (primarily for CBR-related incidents) in response to 9/11. Approximately one-third of law enforcement agencies in both small and large counties did so.

In contrast, law enforcement agencies in smaller counties tended to be less proactively involved in preparedness, consistent with their lower threat perceptions. Only a quarter had done assessments before 9/11, but then worked to catch up after 9/11. Smaller counties tended to rely more on interagency task forces to conduct assessments and to

Table 3.17
Comparison of Law Enforcement in Small Versus Large Counties

Issue	Law Enforcement in Smaller Counties	Law Enforcement in Larger Counties
Approach to terrorism preparedness	Less likely to (a) have specialized terrorism units, (b) to take part in terrorism-related task forces, (c) to have done assessments for their jurisdiction prior to 9/11, (d) to have newly established mutual aid agreements to specifically address terrorist-related incidents.	More likely to (a) be responsible for doing contingency planning for their jurisdiction, (b) take the lead on doing assessments (versus an interagency task force), (c) have done assessments prior to 9/11 and to have done more comprehensive assessments, (d) have specialized terrorism units, (e) take part in terrorism-related task forces, and (f) have developed new mutual aid agreements post 9/11.
Intelligence-related activities	Less likely to (a) have interacted with the FBI's JTTFs, (b) have received counter-terrorism training from the JTTFs, or (c) have received guidance from the FBI about what information should be collected and passed on. Less aware of counterterrorism training offered by their police academy or state government.	More likely to (a) have interacted with the FBI's JTTFs especially to receive counterterrorism training, and (b) have received guidance from the FBI about what information should be collected and passed on. More likely to have coordinated with other federal agencies on terrorist-related investigations during the past five years.
Experience with terrorist-related incidents/ hoaxes	Less likely to have experienced terrorist-related hoaxes or incidents following 9/11. Rated likelihood of occurrence of terrorist threats across most categories as lower.	More likely to have experienced terrorist-related hoaxes or incidents following 9/11. Rated likelihood of occurrence of terrorist threats across most categories as higher.

develop contingency plans for their jurisdiction, suggesting a somewhat different strategy in these counties for addressing preparedness.

Law enforcement agencies in smaller counties were less likely than those in large counties to have

- received guidance from the FBI following 9/11 as to what information to collect and pass on about the terrorist threat
- experience in coordinating with the JTTFs, the FBI, or other federal agencies; when they had interacted with the JTTFs, it was primarily to share intelligence information or to receive counterterrorism training
- made organizational changes to improve their terrorism response capabilities, with less than 5 percent increasing the number of personnel doing emergency response planning following 9/11 and only 14 percent having a specialized terrorism unit.

Law enforcement agencies in smaller counties also tended to view communications interoperability as less of a problem than those located in large counties. Agencies in smaller counties also were less aware of what counterterrorism training was being offered by their police academy or state and of who was responsible for developing contingency plans for their jurisdiction, suggesting a greater need for awareness training for these agencies.

In summary, these results suggest that at the local level, approaches towards addressing terrorism preparedness varies by size of jurisdiction, and we may also expect to see differences in law enforcement's support needs and how they are resourcing their preparedness activities by size of jurisdiction. We examine these issues in detail in the next chapter.

CHAPTER FOUR

Law Enforcement's Support Needs and How They Are Resourcing Preparedness Activities

Introduction

In Chapter Three, we found that many state and local law enforcement agencies had undertaken a number of steps to improve their preparedness for terrorism both before 9/11 and in response to 9/11. In this chapter, we examine what state and local law enforcement view as being their important support needs in order to improve assessment and response capabilities and how they are resourcing their preparedness activities. Specifically, we examine the ways in which the support needs of state and local law enforcement agencies are similar and how they differ. To understand better how law enforcement is resourcing these activities, we first discuss the priority law enforcement agencies assign to investing in terrorism preparedness and the changes, if any, they made in their spending patterns in response to 9/11 in order to focus on terrorism preparedness. Second, we examine the degree to which law enforcement received external funding or resources following 9/11 to help support these activities and from what sources. We conclude with a discussion and summary of key findings.

Analytic Approach

To examine differences in support needs and resourcing activities, we conducted descriptive analyses presenting the weighted results overall to represent the national estimate of local law enforcement agencies—an estimate that accounts for our sample design and for nonresponse bias. In addition, we compare differences between local law enforcement agencies located in large metropolitan counties ("metro") counties (i.e., central counties of metropolitan areas with a population of 1 million or more)[1] and those agencies located in smaller ("non-metro") counties (i.e., counties with a population of less than 1 million).

For state law enforcement organizations, no weighting was necessary since we undertook a census of these organizations. As noted in Chapter One, we used a finite population correction to derive the standard errors for these state-level organizations. (See the discussions in Chapter One and Appendix A.)

Law Enforcement's Support Needs

What Is Needed to Strengthen Assessment Capabilities?

Although many state and local law enforcement agencies had conducted risk or threat assessments between 2000 and 2002 (partly in response to 9/11 and partly due to their participation in domestic preparedness grant programs), most agencies expressed a desire for some type of support to conduct future assessments. Overall, 89 percent (S.E. 5) of state law enforcement agencies and 67 percent (S.E. 13) of local law enforcement agencies indicated a need for some type of support in order to strengthen assessment capabilities (not shown). However, they differed in what they considered to be their most important support need.

Table 4.1 shows the support needs of those agencies that followed our survey instructions to mark only one support area, representing what agencies would consider to be their *most important* support need. Consistent with their higher threat perceptions, nearly half of state law enforcement agencies and a third of law enforcement agencies in large counties said their most important support need was for better intelligence information regarding the terrorist threat or capability, whereas few agencies in small counties indicated a desire for such support (Table 4.1).

---

[1] Definition is based on the Office of Research and Planning, Bureau of Health Professions, Area Resource File, 2000.

Table 4.1
Law Enforcement's Most Important Support Needs for Conducting Future Assessments

Most Important Assessment Support Needs	State Law Enforcement: State LE Orgs. Who Needed Support (%)	Local Law Enforcement: Local LE Orgs. Who Needed Support (%) — Overall	Metro	Non-Metro
Protocols for conducting and/or evaluating assessments	32 (5)	47 (11)	35 (15)	51 (14)
Better intelligence on terrorist threat/capability from federal government	47 (6)	17 (7)	29 (12)	14 (9)
Training on how to do assessments	0	27 (10)	30 (13)	26 (12)
Better inter-departmental coordination and liaison	0	8 (5)	3 (2)	9 (7)
Access to outside consultant expertise	5 (2)	0.5 (0.4)	2 (2)	0
Other	16 (4)	0.3 (0.2)	1 (1)	0

Standard error of the estimate shown in parentheses. For local law enforcement, the overall n = 165.

In addition, about a third of local law enforcement agencies indicated that training on how to conduct assessments was most important. In comparison, no state law enforcement agency indicated a desire for such training. This result may reflect the fact that responsibility for conducting such assessments largely falls to the local level, with the state government's role being more to "roll up" local assessments into a statewide assessment. Alternatively, state law enforcement may feel that they have all the training they need in this area.

Law enforcement agencies at both the state and local levels also desired protocols for conducting or evaluating assessments. This was particularly true for state law enforcement agencies and local law enforcement agencies within smaller counties (Table 4.1). About a third of state law enforcement agencies and half of law enforcement agencies located within smaller counties identified protocols as being their most important support need.

Given differences in assessment strategies between large and small counties,[2] were there differences by size of jurisdiction in law enforcement's support needs? Law enforcement agencies located in smaller counties were more likely than those in large counties to desire protocols for conducting and evaluating assessments but were less likely to desire intelligence information about the terrorist threat (Table 4.1). However, they were similar in their desire for training on how to conduct assessments, with about a quarter of local law enforcement overall rating training as their most important support need.

In addition, the support needs of local law enforcement agencies that *had not conducted* an assessment were similar to those of law enforcement agencies that *had conducted* an assessment (as shown in Table 4.1). That is, local law enforcement agencies that had not conducted an assessment between 2000 and 2002 similarly desired protocols for conducting and/or evaluating assessments (40 percent) and training on how to do these assessments (17 percent) (not shown). However, only 1 percent indicated a desire for better intelligence on the terrorist threat or capability, suggesting perhaps that those law enforcement agencies that had not conducted an assessment tended to view the threat to their jurisdiction as being relatively low (not shown).

What Is Needed to Strengthen Response Capabilities?

The type of support needed to strengthen response capabilities fell into three broad categories: training, equipment, and other types of support. Here we did not limit the respondent to just one option, since we expected that law enforcement agencies may have multiple support needs in more than one area in order to strengthen response capabilities.

In general, state law enforcement agencies and local law enforcement agencies in large counties tended to have a greater number of support needs across the different categories listed in Table 4.2, consistent with their higher threat perceptions (as reported in Chapter Two) and their more proactive engagement in preparedness activities (as reported in Chapter Three). In comparison, law enforcement agencies in

---

[2] That is, responsibility for conducting assessments primarily fell to law enforcement in large counties versus an interagency task force in smaller counties.

Table 4.2
What Does Law Enforcement Need to Strengthen Response Capabilities?

	State Law Enforcement	Local Law Enforcement		
	All State LE	All Local LE Orgs. (%)		
Training Needs	**Orgs. (%)**	**Overall**	**Metro**	**Non-Metro**
Joint operational training	67 (8)	45 (11)	87 (5)	35 (11)
Training on how to operate in hazardous environments	44 (8)	37 (9)	72 (9)	29 (10)
Training on how to conduct/ incorporate lessons learned from exercises	57 (8)	29 (8)	48 (13)	25 (9)
Training on evidence collection	33 (8)	28 (8)	55 (12)	22 (8)
Training on use of incident command system	38 (8)	20 (6)	41 (12)	15 (6)
Equipment Needs		**Overall**	**Metro**	**Non-Metro**
Personal protection equipment (PPE) level C for response personnel	59 (8)	50 (11)	77 (8)	43 (12)
Ppe levels A and B for response personnel	44 (8)	44 (10)	53 (14)	42 (12)
Better sensor technology to rapidly determine hazard	67 (8)	37 (9)	52 (14)	33 (11)
Other Needs		**Overall**	**Metro**	**Non-Metro**
Improved communications systems and interoperability	82 (6)	45 (11)	76 (8)	38 (12)
More/better intelligence information on threats and terrorist activity in region	64 (8)	42 (10)	72 (9)	34 (11)
More manpower dedicated to response planning and/or to counterterrorism activities	87 (5)	35 (9)	45 (13)	33 (10)
Other needs	10 (5)	28 (14)	2 (1)	35 (16)

Standard error of the estimate shown in parentheses.

smaller counties tended to have fewer support needs, consistent with their lower threat perceptions and less-active engagement in preparedness activities.

With respect to training, nearly half of local law enforcement agencies wanted more joint operational training in preparing for, and responding to, terrorist-related incidents (Table 4.2). Nearly 30 percent of local law enforcement agencies desired training on evidence collection and how to conduct tabletop or field exercises: 37 percent desired training on how to operate in hazardous environments (Table 4.2). One out of five local law enforcement agencies desired training on the use of the incident command system. Law enforcement agencies in large counties, in particular, indicated a need for training in each of these areas.

Training support was also important at the state level. About two-thirds of state law enforcement agencies desired more joint operational training and training on how to conduct tabletop, field, and day-after exercises (Table 4.2). Nearly half of state agencies also wanted training on how to operate in a hazardous environment, and about a third desired training on evidence collection and the use of the incident command system.

With respect to equipment needs, about half of local law enforcement agencies desired support for the purchase of Levels A, B, or C PPE for their response personnel and for training on its usage (Table 4.2). A similar percentage of state law enforcement agencies also indicated a need for Levels A, B, and C PPE. Consistent with their desire for training on how to operate in hazardous environments and for more and better PPE, a third of local law enforcement and two-thirds of state law enforcement agencies desired better sensor technology to rapidly identify hazards that their response personnel may encounter.

Manpower needs appeared to be more acute at the state level. Eighty-seven percent of state law enforcement agencies wanted more manpower to enable them to dedicate personnel to response planning and/or counterterrorism activities, as compared to only 35 percent of local law enforcement agencies.

Consistent with their lower ratings as to the adequacy of their communications systems (as seen in Chapter Three), the majority of state law enforcement agencies (82 percent) and local law enforcement agencies located in large counties (76 percent) indicated a need to replace aging communications systems and improve communications interoperability between emergency responders. Also, consistent with their higher threat perceptions, a majority of state law enforcement agencies and local agencies in large counties expressed a desire for better intelligence information about the threat for their region or jurisdiction.

The support needs of law enforcement agencies located in large counties merit highlighting. For all of the categories listed in Table 4.2, law enforcement agencies in large counties expressed more support needs than agencies located within smaller counties. Given these agencies' higher threat perceptions and their more-active engagement in preparedness activities at the local level, this result is not surprising. In addition, as noted above, local law enforcement agencies in large counties were similar to state law enforcement agencies in their desire for support in certain areas (e.g., intelligence information and communications interoperability, training on how to conduct lessons learned, and training on the use of the incident command system). In other areas, law enforcement agencies located in large counties appeared to have greater training and equipment needs than did state law enforcement agencies, specifically in the areas of joint operational training, training on evidence collection and operating in hazardous environments, and the need for more and better PPE.

These results suggest that federal preparedness funding and resources need to be tailored to take into account these differences at the state and local levels in law enforcement's support needs.

How Law Enforcement Is Resourcing Their Preparedness Activities

To better understand how law enforcement agencies were resourcing their preparedness activities and how these compared to other public safety responsibilities, we asked survey respondents (1) how high a priority it was for their agency to spend departmental resources on terrorism preparedness compared to other needs of their agency; (2) whether their agency increased departmental spending or internally reallocated resources following 9/11, and if so, for what purposes; and (3) whether their department received any external funding or resources following 9/11 to support these additional preparedness activities, and if so, from what sources. The results are presented below.

For Many Local Law Enforcement Agencies, Investing Resources on Terrorism Preparedness Was a Low Priority

Compared to other needs of their department, terrorism preparedness was not viewed as a high priority by local law enforcement (Table 4.3). Overall, only 7 percent of local law enforcement agencies rated spending departmental resources on terrorism preparedness a high priority, with 21 percent rating it as only somewhat of a priority. Law enforcement agencies in large counties were more likely than agencies in smaller counties to assign a higher priority rating in each of the categories listed in Table 4.3. Of the 35 percent of law enforcement agencies that indicated it was not at all a priority for their department, almost all were located in smaller counties.[3]

At the state level, sending departmental resources for terrorism preparedness was a higher priority. Nearly half of state law enforcement agencies indicated that it was a high priority, and about a third indicated that it was somewhat of a priority (Table 4.3). None said it was not at all a priority.

Still, a Number of Law Enforcement Agencies Undertook Steps to Improve Preparedness Following 9/11

Although not a high priority at the local level, after 9/11, about a quarter of local law enforcement agencies increased departmental spending or internally reallocated resources to focus on improving their preparedness for terrorism (Table 4.4). Law enforcement agencies in large counties were more likely than those in smaller counties to have internally reallocated agency resources following 9/11 for this purpose (39 percent versus 16 percent). Local law enforcement did so for a variety of reasons, especially to focus on planning activities (development of response plans, participation in interagency planning activities) and on training and exercises. In addition, agencies located in large counties

---

[3] The priority assigned to preparedness compared to other departmental needs has to be interpreted with caution. It is important to keep in mind that the public-safety mission of law enforcement agencies is broad, including crime prevention, response, and investigation. Further, one might expect that law enforcement agencies in large counties might have a wider range of public-safety duties they have to be concerned about, in addition to terrorism preparedness, than law enforcement agencies in smaller counties.

Table 4.3
How High a Priority Do Law Enforcement Agencies Assign Spending Departmental Resources on Terrorism Preparedness?

	State Law Enforcement	Local Law Enforcement		
		All Local LE Orgs. (%)		
Priority Rating	**All State LE Orgs. (%)**	**Overall**	**Metro**	**Non-Metro**
High priority	49 (4)	7 (3)	14 (7)	5 (3)
Somewhat of a priority	33 (4)	21 (6)	31 (10)	18 (7)
Low priority	18 (3)	37 (10)	54 (13)	33 (11)
Not at all a priority	0	35 (13)	0.1 (0.1)	44 (15)

Standard error of the estimate shown in parentheses.

increased spending or reallocated resources following 9/11 in order to provide additional security for their department and to conduct needs and risk or threat assessments (Table 4.4).

Investing departmental resources on terrorism preparedness was a higher priority for state law enforcement agencies, with 51 percent increasing departmental spending and 64 percent internally reallocating agency resources following 9/11 for this purpose (Table 4.4). They did so for a wider variety of reasons as compared to local law enforcement. About two-thirds of state law enforcement agencies increased spending or internally reallocated resources following 9/11 in order to support interagency planning and coordination activities, develop or modify response plans, and further train personnel. In addition, nearly half of state law enforcement agencies did so in order to establish specialized terrorism units, undertake training exercises, and purchase equipment.

Few Local Agencies Received External Funding Following 9/11

Although terrorism preparedness was not a high priority at the local level, following 9/11 some agencies undertook steps to improve their terrorism preparedness, especially those located in large counties. Yet, as shown in Table 4.5, only one out of five local law enforcement agencies reported having received external funding following 9/11 to support these additional activities. Further, there were no significant differences

Table 4.4
Following 9/11, Did Law Enforcement Agencies Increase Spending on Terrorism Preparedness?

	State Law Enforcement	Local Law Enforcement		
		All Local LE Orgs (%)		
Did Department . . .	**All State LE Orgs. (%)**	**Overall**	**Metro**	**Non-Metro**
Internally increase spending?	51 (4)	26 (8)	31 (10)	24 (9)
Internally reallocate resources?	64 (4)	21 (6)	39 (11)	16 (7)
		All Local LE Orgs. (%)		
Purpose?	**All State LE Orgs. (%)**	**Overall**	**Metro**	**Non-Metro**
Additional training of personnel	59 (4)	28 (8)	44 (12)	25 (9)
Develop response plans	64 (4)	23 (7)	32 (10)	21 (8)
Support interagency planning and coordination activities	62 (4)	21 (7)	26 (9)	19 (8)
Conduct or participate in tabletop or field exercises	46 (4)	19 (6)	38 (11)	15 (6)
Purchase specialized equipment (e.g., PPE, sensors)	46 (4)	17 (6)	18 (6)	17 (7)
Increase security for department	38 (4)	13 5)	25 (9)	10 (5)
Conduct a needs assessment	44 (4)	12 (5)	28 (9)	8 (5)
Conduct risk or threat assessment	36 (4)	12 (5)	22 (8)	9 (5)
Cover staff overtime	33 (4)	11 (5)	14 (6)	10 (5)
Establish specialized units	46 (4)	6 (3)	10 (6)	5 (4)

Standard error of the estimate shown in parentheses.

between law enforcement agencies in large versus smaller counties with respect to receipt of external funding or resources following 9/11. Of those that did receive such support, the primary sources were the federal government and their state's OEM. In addition, 9 percent received support from their city or county government.

For state law enforcement agencies, it was a much different story. Nearly two-thirds reported receiving external funding or resources following 9/11 to support their preparedness activities (Table 4.5). As indicated above, their preparedness activities covered a broader range of areas than did those of local law enforcement. The primary source of funding for state law enforcement agencies was the federal government. Fifty-one percent of state law enforcement agencies reported receiving funding or other support from the federal government following 9/11 (Table 4.5). Also, 15 percent of state law enforcement agencies received funding from their state's OEM, and 10 percent from other state agencies.

Discussion

Law Enforcement's Support Needs For Conducting Future Assessments

Although many state and local law enforcement agencies had conducted threat or risk assessments in response to 9/11 (or as part of U.S. domestic preparedness programs), most expressed a desire for some

Table 4.5
Following 9/11, Did Law Enforcement Agencies Receive External Funding or Resources to Support Terrorism Preparedness Activities?

	State Law Enforcement	Local Law Enforcement		
		All Local LE Orgs. (%)		
Receive External Funding or Resources?	All State LE Orgs. (%)	Overall	Metro	Non-Metro
Yes	59 (4)	20 (6)	23 (8)	20 (7)
		All Local LE Orgs. (%)		
Source(s)?	All State LE Orgs. (%)	Overall	Metro	Non-Metro
Federal government	51 (4)	12 (5)	9 (4)	13 (6)
State OEM (or equivalent)	15 (3)	7 (3)	9 (4)	6 (4)
Other state agencies	10 (2)	0.3 (0.2)	2 (1)	0
Local OEM (or equivalent)	n/a	3 (1)	3 (2)	3 (2)
City or county	n/a	3 (2)	9 (5)	2 (2)

Standard error of the estimate shown in parentheses.

type of support to help them conduct future assessments. However, what they considered to be their most important support need in this area differed somewhat. Nearly half of state law enforcement agencies and a third of local law enforcement agencies in large counties desired better intelligence information regarding the terrorist threat or capability, consistent with their higher threat perceptions. In comparison, few law enforcement agencies located in smaller counties desired this type of support, also consistent with their lower threat perceptions.

Instead, law enforcement agencies in smaller counties, in particular, desired protocols for conducting or evaluating assessments. About a third of state law enforcement agencies also identified protocols as being their most important support need.

Training on how to conduct assessments was desired by about a third of local law enforcement agencies in both large and small counties. However, none of the state law enforcement agencies indicated a need for such training, perhaps reflecting the fact that responsibility for doing such assessments falls primarily to the local level, with state government's role being more to "roll up" local assessments into a statewide assessment. Alternatively, state law enforcement agencies may feel that they have adequate training in doing assessments and do not see this as being an important support area.

Law Enforcement's Support Needs for Improving Response Capabilities

To improve response capabilities, law enforcement's support needs fell into three broad categories: training, equipping, and other types of support.

In general, state law enforcement agencies and local law enforcement agencies within large counties had a greater number of support needs in each of these three areas and were somewhat similar in the type of support they desired, consistent with their higher threat perceptions (as reported in Chapter Two) and their more proactive engagement in preparedness activities (as reported in Chapter Three). In contrast, local law enforcement agencies within smaller counties tended to have fewer support needs, also consistent with their lower threat perceptions and less-active engagement in preparedness activities.

With respect to training, a majority of state law enforcement agencies desired support in the areas of joint operations, conducting field or tabletop exercises, and incorporating lessons learned from exercises. In addition, about half desired training on operating in a hazardous environment, and about a third desired training on evidence collection and the use of the incident command system.

Law enforcement agencies in large counties were similar to state agencies in their desire for training on the use of the incident command system and on incorporating lessons learned from exercises. However, law enforcement agencies in large counties appeared to have greater training and equipment support needs than state law enforcement agencies in the areas of joint operations, evidence collection, operating in a hazardous environment, and more and better PPE.

The appropriate use of PPE by law enforcement personnel merits further discussion, with this also possibly being an area for greater awareness training. About half of state and local law enforcement agencies desired support to purchase Levels A or B PPE; two-thirds or more also desired Level C PPE. These survey results reflect an incomplete understanding by state and local law enforcement of the purpose of the different levels of PPE and the mission(s) of law enforcement in a hazardous-environment situation. Typically, hazardous-materials (HAZMAT) units or personnel from the fire department or health department will be required to operate in a HAZMAT environment. There are four levels of protective clothing ensembles to be worn when dealing with hazardous materials, with Level A PPE providing the greatest level of protection.[4] Only a limited number of law enforce-

---

[4] Level A suits fully encapsulate the body so that no vapor penetrates the suit; respiratory protection is provided through supplied air (such as a self-contained breathing apparatus [SCBA]). Level B suits are full-body, chemical-resistant suits that may introduce vapors; respiratory protection and other protection features are normally the same as with a Level A suit. Level C suits are full-body chemical suits with the same properties as Level B suits, except that an air-purifying respirator is used instead of supplied-air respiratory protection. Level D suits protect against contact exposure only, and no respiratory protection is required. (The RAND 2002 survey did not ask about Level D suits.) T. LaTourrette, D. J. Peterson, J. T. Bartis, and B. A. Jackson, *Protecting Emergency Responders*, Vol. 2: *Community Views of Safety and Health Risks and Personal Protection Needs,* Santa Monica, Calif.: RAND Corporation, MR-1646-NIOSH, 2003.

ment personnel and agencies will operate in a "hot" zone and thus require Level A PPE. Level B PPE is appropriate for conducting a force-protection mission in a "warm" zone, whereas Level C PPE would be used by law enforcement personnel in the outer perimeter. All levels of PPE have a limit on how long an individual can operate in the protective ensemble, and it would be rare for all on-duty law enforcement staff to require this type of protection.[5] The fact that so many state and law enforcement agencies indicated a support need for all types of PPE either reflects a lack of understanding regarding its application or may reflect in part problems with grant-distribution mechanisms. That is, first-responder grant and funding timelines, in some instances, have been compressed, with local law enforcement given short turnaround times to apply for grant funds being distributed by state governments. Anecdotal evidence suggests that compressed grant deadlines and timelines for spending of funds have resulted in a rush to purchase equipment without adequate time, in some cases, for individual departments to assess their equipment needs. Further, a limitation of some grant programs has been that they provide support to purchase equipment, but not necessarily to hire personnel.

Other support needs expressed included the need for better intelligence information, particularly important to state law enforcement agencies and local law enforcement within larger counties. For example, about two-thirds of state law enforcement agencies and three-quarters of law enforcement agencies located in large counties desired better intelligence information about the threat to and terrorist activities within their region, whereas only a third of local law enforcement agencies in smaller counties desired such support.

Consistent with their lower ratings as to the adequacy of their public safety communications systems (as seen in Chapter Three), the majority of state law enforcement agencies (82 percent) and law enforcement agencies located in large counties (76 percent) also indicated

---

[5] The Office for Domestic Preparedness (ODP), as an entity of the Department of Justice (DOJ) under the Office of Justice Programs (OJP) prior to the creation of DHS, administered the 2001 equipment grant program. These were direct grants (not reimbursements) for planning, training, equipment, and exercises. Many of the initial orders for PPE occurred as part of the Fiscal Year 2001 equipment grant program process.

a need to replace aging communications systems and to improve communications interoperability.

In the survey, we purposely did not ask whether funding was an important support need, since we expected the majority of law enforcement respondents to indicate this to be the case. Instead, we felt a more informative question would be to ask survey respondents to indicate which of different types of support were needed in order to strengthen their agency's assessment and response capabilities. The fact that so few local law enforcement agencies reported receiving external funding or resources following 9/11 suggests that many would have identified funding as a critical shortfall. Indeed, some survey respondents in their written comments wrote down funding (for training, personnel [including overtime], and equipment) as one of the three areas in which their department was weakest.

How Law Enforcement Is Resourcing Preparedness Activities

For many local law enforcement agencies, investing departmental resources on terrorism preparedness was a low priority compared to other needs of their department. Although a low priority, about a quarter of local law enforcement agencies increased departmental spending or internally reallocated resources following 9/11 to improve their response capabilities. They did so primarily to undertake planning and training activities with few (one out of five) receiving external funding or resources after 9/11 to support these preparedness activities. Of those that did, the primary sources of support were the federal government or their state's OEM.

Law enforcement agencies located in large counties placed greater importance on terrorism preparedness than those located in smaller counties. For example, 45 percent of law enforcement agencies in large counties rated investing departmental resources on terrorism preparedness as a high priority or somewhat of a priority for their agency. More of these law enforcement agencies also internally reallocated resources following 9/11 to focus on terrorism preparedness than did agencies in smaller counties (39 percent versus 16 percent). They did so not only to do planning and training activities, but also to conduct needs and risk or threat assessments and to provide additional security for their department. Although terrorism preparedness was a higher priority for law enforcement agencies located within large counties, and they tended to be more proactive in improving response capabilities following 9/11, we found no differences between law enforcement agencies located in large versus smaller counties in the receipt of external funding or resources after 9/11 to support these additional activities.

These survey results raise the question of what perhaps was not getting done at the local level. That is, following 9/11, what sort of public safety activities may have been sacrificed as a result of shifting resources or personnel to focus on terrorism preparedness and response? One can make the argument that emergency preparedness for terrorism may go hand in hand with law enforcement's other public safety duties. Thus, it may be that nothing in the system was sacrificed. Yet these results suggest that in taking on these additional demands, some local departments may have been stretched thin during that first year following 9/11.

For state law enforcement agencies it was a much different story. Investing departmental resources on terrorism preparedness was a greater priority, with 49 percent of state law enforcement agencies saying it was a high priority for their department and 33 percent indicating it was somewhat of a priority.

Following 9/11, about half of state law enforcement agencies increased departmental spending, and about two-thirds internally reallocated resources to focus on terrorism preparedness. They did so for a wider variety of reasons than local law enforcement alone. About two-thirds of state law enforcement agencies increased spending or reallocated resources to support interagency planning and coordination activities, development or modification of response plans, or additional training of personnel. About half did so in order to establish specialized terrorism units, participate in training exercises, or purchase equipment.

Unlike local law enforcement, the majority of state law enforcement agencies received external funding following 9/11, primarily from the federal government, to support these activities. The higher percentage of state law enforcement agencies that received funding after 9/11 as compared to local law enforcement may reflect in part the shift that occurred from federal grants being distributed directly to the local level now going through the state governments. In addition, some of this funding may have been used to provide training of local law enforcement and other first responders as well as to participate in planning activities.

Soon after 9/11, ODP made available about $800 million in federal preparedness funding to the first-responder community. In addition, many state and local city and county governments also increased spending on terrorism preparedness, with some of that funding going to law enforcement. However, distribution of funds takes time. By the time of our survey in fall 2002, it may have been that only a portion of this funding had been distributed to the law enforcement community.

Since our 2002 survey, it is likely that more law enforcement agencies have received external funding to support their terrorism preparedness activities. However, the evidence suggests that many law enforcement agencies have received only modest support to date due to several reasons. A recent report by the DHS Inspector General's Office on the distribution and spending of ODP first-responder grant funds found that the receipt and spending of these funds has been slow. For example, as of February 2004, the majority of the $882 million in the FY 2002 State Domestic Preparedness Program (SDPP) and FY 2003 SHSGP first-responder grant funds awarded by ODP still remained in the U.S. Treasury.[6] The majority of the $1.5 billion awarded in FY 2003 SHSGP Part II had also not been distributed. By February 2004, of the $316 million in FY 2002 SDPP funds awarded, only 36 percent of awards had been drawn down.

In addition, the nation's renewed focus on improving domestic preparedness for terrorism following 9/11 came at a time when many state, county, and city governments were experiencing severe fiscal crises. Faced with projected budget gaps and declining revenues, state and local governments have had to make some difficult decisions in attempting to balance budgets and reduce overall expenditures. Further, investments in terrorism preparedness have had to compete with other local priorities. A 2002 survey of 725 city officials on the most important issues confronting their cities found that terrorism ranked fourth

---

[6] DHS, Office of the Inspector General, "An Audit of Distributing and Spending 'First-Responder' Grant Funds," Report No. OIG-04-15 March 2004.

behind public safety, the local economy, and infrastructure repair and development.[7]

It is important to keep in mind that these survey results are based on self-reported information. We were unable to independently verify whether an agency received external funding or resources following 9/11 or the amount of funding received. We only asked survey respondents whether their department had received any funding or resources following 9/11, and if so, from what source. We did not ask about the amount of funding received or what proportion of their department's total budget it represented.

Variation in Support Needs and Resourcing of Preparedness Activities by Size of County

Table 4.6 compares law enforcement agencies located within large counties (i.e., counties with a population of 1 million or more) with those within smaller counties in terms of their support needs to improve assessment and response capabilities and how they are resourcing preparedness activities.

Consistent with their higher threat perceptions, law enforcement agencies in large counties were more likely than those in smaller counties to desire better intelligence information regarding the terrorist threat or capability in their jurisdiction or region.

Smaller counties had less experience in conducting assessments, and in particular desired protocols on how to do so. Law enforcement agencies in large and small counties were similar, though, in their desire for training on how to conduct assessments.

In general, law enforcement agencies within large counties had a wider range of support needs to improve response capabilities than those agencies located in smaller counties. The differences between local law enforcement within large versus small counties in their support needs was striking. In general, more than twice as many law enforce-

---

[7] The National League of Cities survey of 725 city officials was conducted in July and August 2002. Of the most important issues confronting their cities, 62 percent of officials cited public safety, 55 percent cited the local economy, 44 percent cited improving infrastructure, and 34 percent cited terrorism. National League of Cities, "Homeland Security and America's Cities," Research Brief on America's Cities, December 2002.

Table 4.6
Comparison of Law Enforcement's Support Needs in Small Versus Large Counties

Issue	Law Enforcement in Smaller Counties	Law Enforcement in Larger Counties
Support needs to do risk/threat assessments	More likely to want protocols, but similar in desire for training on how to conduct assessments.	Less likely to want protocols, but similar in desire for training on how to conduct assessments. Want better intelligence and information from the federal government on the threat.
Support needs to improve response capabilities	Less likely to want joint operational training or training on evidence collection, use of the incident command system, operating in hazardous environments, or incorporating lessons learned from exercises. Want basic PPE but less likely to desire more specialized PPE or sensor technology. Less likely to view improvements in communications systems and interoperability as important.	More likely to want joint operational training and training on evidence collection, use of the incident command system, operating in hazardous environments, and on incorporating lessons learned from exercises. Want basic PPE and nearly half want more specialized PPE. Want better sensor technology to rapidly identify hazards their response personnel may encounter.
How resourcing preparedness activities	Less likely to (a) assign a high priority to investing in terrorism preparedness, (b) internally reallocate agency resources after 9/11 to focus on terrorism preparedness. Similar in percentage of agencies (20%) that received external funding following 9/11 to support preparedness activities.	More likely to (a) assign a higher priority to investing in terrorism preparedness, or (b) internally reallocate agency resources after 9/11 to focus on terrorism preparedness. Similar in the percentage of agencies that received external funding following 9/11 to support preparedness activities.

ment agencies in large counties as in smaller counties indicated support needs in each of the categories we asked about, with only a few exceptions. For example, whereas 87 percent of law enforcement agencies within large counties desired joint operational training, only 35 percent of agencies in smaller counties indicated a need for such support. However, they were similar in their desire for PPE, with roughly half of law enforcement agencies in small and large counties indicating a need for Levels A or B PPE. Overall, law enforcement agencies in smaller counties expressed fewer support needs.

In terms of resourcing preparedness activities, law enforcement agencies in large counties tended to assign a higher priority to investing resources in terrorism preparedness and were more likely than agencies located in smaller counties to internally reallocate departmental resources after 9/11 to focus on preparedness. However, law enforcement agencies in large and small counties were similar with respect to the receipt of external funding or resources following 9/11. Only one out of five agencies reported receiving external support in the year following the 9/11 terrorist attacks.

CHAPTER FIVE

Understanding the Relationship Between Risk, Size of Jurisdiction, Receipt of Funding, and Preparedness Activities

Introduction

In Chapters Two and Three, we reported that law enforcement agencies in large counties tended to assess the threat of future terrorist attacks as being greater for their jurisdiction and were more proactive in improving their preparedness for terrorism than those agencies located in smaller counties. In other words, both threat perceptions and preparedness activities of law enforcement appear to be correlated with size of jurisdiction.

However, the relationship between threat perceptions, preparedness activities, size of jurisdiction, and receipt of funding appears to be a complex one. Although spending resources on terrorism preparedness was not a high priority at the local level, a number of these law enforcement agencies (particularly those in large counties) undertook various steps to improve their level of preparedness and response capabilities following 9/11. However, relatively few law enforcement agencies (one out of five) reported receiving external funding or resources in the year following 9/11 to support these activities, consistent with the DHS Office of the Inspector General's report findings of significant delays since 9/11 in the distribution and spending of first-responder grant funds from the federal and state to the local levels.[1]

Further, we found no difference between law enforcement agencies located in large counties versus those in smaller counties with re-

[1] DHS, Office of the Inspector General, "An Audit of Distributing and Spending 'First-Responder' Grant Funds," Report No. OIG-04-15, March 2004.

spect to the receipt of funding or resources following 9/11, suggesting little or no relationship between size of jurisdiction and receipt of funding (and, by inference, no significant relationship between threat perceptions and receipt of funding). That is, although law enforcement agencies in large counties tended to perceive the threat as being greater for their jurisdiction and were more proactive in undertaking preparedness activities both before and after 9/11, they were not more successful than law enforcement agencies located in smaller counties in obtaining external funding following 9/11.

Threat is just one dimension of risk, however, with level of vulnerability being another key dimension. Further, threat is difficult to quantify for a particular jurisdiction and may vary over time. Therefore, we felt that risk would be a more robust measure to use in examining these relationships. The survey provided us with information on what physical vulnerabilities exist within these different jurisdictions and regions.

To better understand the relationship between level of risk, size of jurisdiction, receipt of funding, and preparedness activities (see Figure 5.1), we developed a measure of perceived risk utilizing information from the survey on threat perceptions and on physical vulnerabilities. Specifically, we were interested in addressing the following questions:

- Were law enforcement agencies that received external funding following 9/11 more likely than those that did not to undertake steps to improve their level of preparedness?
- Were law enforcement agencies that perceived the risk of terrorist attacks to be higher for their jurisdiction more likely than those that perceived the risk to be lower to undertake steps to improve their level of preparedness following 9/11?
- What is the relationship between level of perceived risk and size of jurisdiction?
- What is the relationship between level of perceived risk and receipt of funding?

In this chapter, we first discuss the analytic approach we used to develop a measure of perceived risk and to analyze the relationships

Figure 5.1
Relationship Between Perceived Level of Risk, Size of Jurisdiction, Preparedness Activities, and Funding

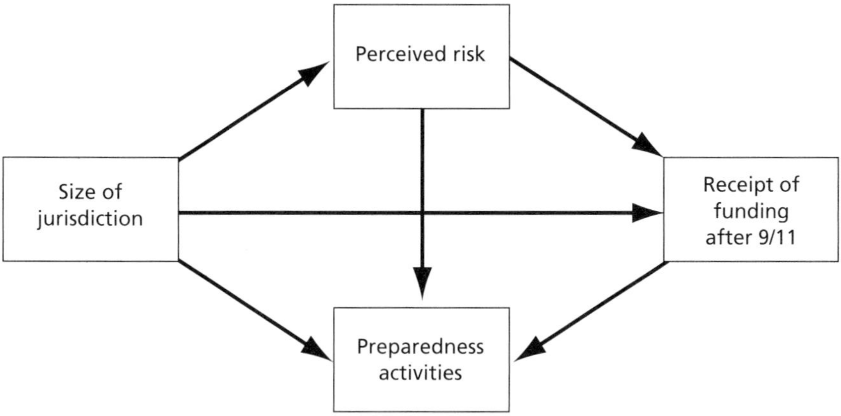

RAND *MG104-5.1*

between level of risk, size of jurisdiction, receipt of funding, and preparedness activities. Second, we present the results of our analyses in four areas: (1) relationship between receipt of funding and preparedness activities, (2) relationship between level of perceived risk and preparedness activities, (3) relationship between level of perceived risk and size of jurisdiction, and (4) relationship between level of perceived risk and receipt of funding. We conclude with a discussion of the identified relationships and a summary of key findings.

Analytic Approach

Assessing Relationship Between the Perception of Risk and Undertaking Preparedness Activities

To see if there were differences between local law enforcement agencies in their preparedness activities based on agencies' perceptions regarding the risk of terrorism, we constructed a measure of perceived risk. Risk can be defined as having two components: *threat* and *vulnerability*. In the survey, we included two questions that could serve as proxies for measuring perceived threat and level of vulnerability. Our goal was to create these individual measures of perceived threat and level of vulnerability and then combine them into a single qualitative measure of *risk*. We describe the process we used below.

In terms of perceived threat, Question 1 on the survey asked respondents to rate the likelihood of eight different types of major terrorist incidents occurring within their jurisdiction or region within the next five years. The eight types of incidents were chemical, biological, radiological, cyberterrorism, conventional-explosives incident, agroterrorism involving a food contaminant, agroterrorism involving animal disease, and an incident involving the use of military-grade weapons.[2] For each type of incident, respondents were asked to rate the likelihood of that incident occurring in their jurisdiction or region within the next five years on a scale of 1 to 4, where 1 = very unlikely, 2 = somewhat unlikely, 3 = somewhat likely, and 4 = very likely. Table 5.1 shows the distribution of responses for each incident type.

In general, for each incident type, we found that approximately 50 percent of organizations rated it as very unlikely, except for conventional explosives, where only 26 percent rated it as very unlikely. At the other end of the scale, very few organizations (between 1 and 4 percent) rated it as highly likely for any of the incident types listed in Table 5.1. Between 30 and 40 percent of organizations rated the likelihood of occurrence as somewhat unlikely for the incident types presented, except for conventional explosives, where 55 percent rated it somewhat unlikely. Between 8 and 18 percent of organizations rated the likelihood of occurrence for the incident types listed as being somewhat likely.

To create a measure of perceived threat using the information in Question 1, we also had to take into account the possible pattern of scores across the eight incident types in considering how to define our low, medium, and high-threat groups. We summed up the individual scores on each item to assign an overall threat score for an organization. The possible scores on the scale ranged in theory from 8 (where a respondent rated all eight incident types as very unlikely) to 32 (where a respondent rated all eight incident types as very likely).

---

[2] Military-grade weapons included automatic weapons, mortars, etc.

Table 5.1
Percieved Likelihood of Different Types of Terrorist Incidents Occurring Within Jurisdiction or Region Within the Next Five Years

	All Local Law Enforcement Orgs. (%)			
Incident Type	Very Unlikely	Somewhat Unlikely	Somewhat Likely	Very Likely
Chemical	54 (11)	29 (8)	13 (5)	4 (3)
Biological	52 (11)	31 (9)	15 (6)	2 (1)
Radiological	53 (11)	38 (10)	8 (4)	1 (1)
Cyberterrorism	51 (11)	28 (8)	18 (6)	3 (1)
Conventional explosives	26 (9)	55 (11)	17 (6)	2 (1)
Military-grade weapons (e.g., mortars, automatic weapons)	50 (11)	40 (10)	9 (4)	1 (1)
Agroterrorism involving food contaminants	47 (12)	40 (10)	13 (5)	0[a]
Agroterrorism involving animal disease	52 (11)	34 (9)	13 (5)	1

Standard error of the estimate shown in parentheses.
[a]Less than 1 percent.

First, we designated respondents who rated all eight incident types as very likely as being in the low-threat group (i.e., a score of 8). The next problem was to define the boundary between the low- and medium-threat groups. We thought of two prototypical questionnaire responses for Question 1 that could be the boundary between the low and medium groups in perceived threat. We considered how many incident types respondents would have to be rated as somewhat unlikely to be considered a medium-threat group. On Question 1, the median score was 12 (i.e., 50 percent of all law enforcement agencies had scores equal to or less than 12). In this case, the median would be equivalent to a respondent rating four incident types as somewhat unlikely and four incident types as very unlikely on Question 1. Given this, we decided to use the median, a score of 12, as the boundary between the low- and medium-threat groups, with a score of 12 placing an organization into the low-threat group.

Second, we needed to define the high-threat group. As noted above, very few organizations rated any incidents as very likely. Thus, we focused instead on the *somewhat likely* category, considering how many items respondents would have had to rate as somewhat likely to be considered a high-threat group. We felt that those respondents that rated all eight incident types as somewhat likely (i.e., a score of 24) would clearly fall into the high-threat group.

Third, we had to define the boundary between the medium- and high-threat groups. Using a score of 20 as the upper bound for the medium group would be equivalent to an organization rating four incident types as somewhat likely and four incident types as somewhat unlikely. An alternative criterion would be to select the top 10 percent of scores as being the high-threat group. Based on this second criterion, we defined the high-threat group as those organizations with a score of 21 or greater. Thus, scores between 13 and 20 were defined as our medium-threat group.

Fourth, we had 12 cases that were missing a likelihood value for one of the eight incident types and 3 cases that had a missing value for two of the incident types. To impute the missing values for these 15 cases, we fitted a random effects model to the entire data set:

$$y\_ij = a\_i + b\_j + e$$

where y_ij is the jth response for person i; a_i is a person-level effect (that will be small for those cases that tended to rate the likelihood value for the non-missing incident types as very unlikely or somewhat unlikely); and b_j is a variable-level effect (that will be large for those cases that more frequently rated the likelihood for the non-missing incident types as somewhat likely or very likely). Effectively, the imputed value for a particular missing y_ij will be similar to the average of other respondents' answers to question j, but pulled toward person i's average response across the questions.

Finally, one case skipped Question 1 entirely and so was omitted from the analysis. Table 5.2 displays the three categories defined for our perceived-threat measure using the above decision rules.

For the threat measure, we also looked at the characteristics of local law enforcement agencies surveyed that may affect their threat categorization. To do so, we fitted a logistic regression model to try to distinguish between low-threat agencies and medium- or high-threat

Table 5.2
Perceived-Threat Measure

Threat Categories	Sum of Scores	Criterion
Low perceived threat	8–12	Median (50% of organizations fell into this range)
Medium perceived threat	13–20	40% of organizations fell into this range
High perceived threat	21–32	Top 10% of organizations

agencies. Our model included indicators for metro and non-metro counties, size of department, and census region. We found no differences between agencies in metro and non-metro counties. Both department size and census region, however, were predictive of the chance of an agency being in the medium- or high-threat category. The odds of being in the medium- or high-threat category were more than nine times higher for law enforcement agencies with more than 30 officers than for agencies with less than 30 officers. After adjusting for metro and non-metro locality and department size, we found that law enforcement agencies in census region 3 (South) and census region 4 (West) were most likely to be in the low-threat category, while the odds of an agency being in the medium- or high-threat category were nine times higher for agencies in census region 1 (Northeast) and census region 2 (Midwest), with census region 1 reporting the greatest threat. (See Appendix B for the logistic regression results.)

Next, to create our measure of vulnerability, we used information from Question 7 on the survey about the types of facilities that local law enforcement agencies had located within their jurisdiction or region that might be considered potential targets for a terrorist attack. We created our measure of vulnerability based on the distribution of the number of types of facilities that agencies indicated were located within their jurisdiction or region. The distribution breakdown shown in Table 5.3 shows the criteria we used to define our low, medium, and high-vulnerability groups. Approximately a third of law enforcement agencies indicated they had none of the types of facilities listed in Question 7 within their jurisdiction, another third indicated they had between one and three, and a little more than a third indicated they had four or more.

Using these two measures of perceived threat and vulnerability, we constructed a qualitative measure of risk, building a three-by-three

Table 5.3
Vulnerablitiy Measure

Vulnerability Categories	Types of Facilities Located in Jurisdiction	Distribution of All Local Law Enforcement Orgs. (%)
Low vulnerability	0	27
Medium vulnerability	1–3	33
High vulnerability	4+	40

matrix where we arrayed along one axis our categorical measure of perceived threat and along the other axis our categorical measure of vulnerability (Figure 5.2). We defined the high-risk group as those organizations that were high on both perceived threat and vulnerability or medium on one and high on the other. We defined the low-risk group as those organizations that were low on both perceived threat and vulnerability or medium on one and low on the other. It was possible to be high on one dimension of risk (e.g., perceived threat) yet low on the other dimension of risk (e.g., vulnerability). Thus, we used the decision rule that the medium-risk group would be those organizations that fell into the medium category for both perceived threat and vulnerability or who were high on one dimension but low on the other. Table 5.4 shows the resulting distribution of cases across the different levels of perceived risk for this measure constructed using the above-described procedure. Roughly a third of organizations fell into each of the perceived-risk categories of low, medium, and high.

Using our measure of perceived risk, we then compared organizations along a series of preparedness activities and conducted chi-square tests to assess statistical significance. For each of the preparedness activities, we tested whether there was a relationship between a particular preparedness activity and our measure of perceived risk. Most of the questions regarding preparedness activities had yes or no answers. For these activities we fitted logistic regression models estimating the percentage of agencies that had performed that activity for each risk level. We then used an F-test to test for differences in the rates across the three risk levels. Two questions, one concerning when an assessment

Figure 5.2
Qualitative Measure of Perceived Risk

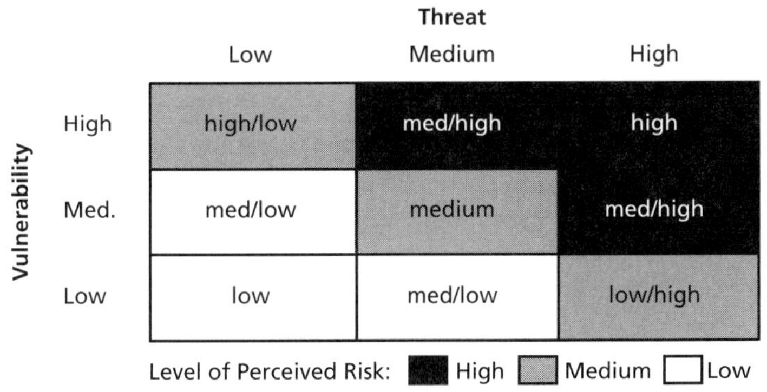

RAND *MG104-5.2*

took place and another concerning the priority of preparedness spending, had more than two levels (i.e., they were not yes-or-no questions per se, but rather had more than two possible response options). For these we used a chi-square test of independence, correcting for the survey weighting.

Assessing Relationship Between Receiving External Funding or Support Following 9/11 and Undertaking Preparedness Activities

To understand better whether receipt of external funding or resources following 9/11 was related to steps taken to improve preparedness (compared to other law enforcement agencies that had not received such support), we compared responses to the question on the survey about receipt of external funding and support following 9/11 with responses to a select set of objective indicators of preparedness. These indicators fell into four broad categories: (1) shifting agency spending or resources to focus on

Table 5.4
Overall Distribution for Measure of Perceived Risk

Level of Perceived Risk	Distribution of All Local Law Enforcement Orgs. (%)
Low	38
Medium	31
High	31

terrorism preparedness; (2) updating written response plans, SOPs, or mutual aid agreements; (3) having specialized units to address terrorism preparedness; (4) participating in training exercises; and (5) assigning higher priority to spending departmental resources on preparedness.

Specifically, we created a categorical variable based on organizations' response to the survey question "Since September 11th, 2001, has your department received an increase in its funding and/or resources from outside of your department (e.g., equipment, training, manpower) specifically for counter- or anti-terrorism purposes?"[3] We then compared those law enforcement agencies that had received external funding or support and those agencies that had not along a series of preparedness activities to assess whether there was a relationship between receiving external funding or support and undertaking preparedness activities. We present the results for all organizations. In some cases there was a skip pattern: a *no* answer to a prior question would ask the respondent to skip a set of more detailed questions relevant only to those respondents that gave a *yes* answer. For those organizations without responses to the detailed questions because of skip patterns, we coded their answers as *no*.

We fitted logistic regression models. Each model used a single indicator of preparedness activities to predict receipt of funding or support. Comparisons were made using logistic regression to test differences between groups for indicators with only two categories; a chi-square test of independence was applied for indicators that had three or more categories. We used standard linearization methods to adjust the standard errors for the sample design and for nonresponse. If the coefficient was significantly different from zero, then we concluded that there was an association between receipt of funding or support and the specific preparedness activity being considered.

---

[3] Question 31 in the law enforcement survey.

Results

Law Enforcement Agencies That Received External Funding Following 9/11 Were More Likely to Undertake Preparedness Activities to Improve Their Response Capabilities

Receipt of external funding (or resources) following 9/11 was predictive of taking steps to improve one's level of preparedness. Specifically, law enforcement agencies that received external funding (or resources) following 9/11 were more likely than other law enforcement agencies to self-report having (1) increased spending or internally reallocated resources to focus on terrorism preparedness after 9/11, (2) a specialized terrorism unit, (3) updated response plans or SOPs after 9/11 for one or more types of terrorism-related incidents, (4) conducted joint training exercises with terrorism-related task forces after 9/11, (5) conducted risk or threat assessments, and (6) assigned a higher priority to expending resources on terrorism preparedness (Tables 5.5, 5.6, and 5.7).

For example, as shown in Table 5.5, 27 percent of local law enforcement agencies overall updated their response plans or SOPs to address terrorist-related incidents following 9/11, with most of this being done for CBR-related incidents. However, of those law enforcement agencies that had received an increase in funding or support, 54 percent also updated their response plans, whereas among local law enforcement agencies that had not received an increase in funding or support, only 20 percent updated their response plans following 9/11.

In addition, law enforcement agencies that received external funding following 9/11 were more likely to increase departmental spending and to reallocate resources to focus on terrorism preparedness (Table 5.5). For example, in response to 9/11, 26 percent of local law enforcement agencies overall increased spending on terrorism preparedness, and 21 percent of agencies internally reallocated resources to focus on terrorism preparedness. However, law enforcement agencies that had received funding were much more likely to have done so than agencies that had not received funding. That is, 49 percent of local law

Table 5.5
Relationship Between Receipt of External Funding or Support and Preparedness Activites

Preparedness Activities	All Local LE Orgs. (%)	Local LE Orgs. That Received Funding or Other Support (%)	Local LE Orgs. That Did Not Receive Funding or Other Support (%)
Following 9/11, internally increased spending	26 (8)	49[a] (14)	20 (8)
Following 9/11, internally reallocated resources	21 (6)	66[b] (13)	9 (3)
Agency has specialized unit responsible for addressing terrorism preparedness	16 (5)	33[a] (11)	12 (5)
Following 9/11 has conducted joint training exercises	13 (4)	30[b] (10)	13 (4)
Following 9/11, updated response plans or SOPs to address terrorism-related incidents[c]	27 (7)	54[b] (14)	20 (7)
Following 9/11, updated existing mutual aid agreements for terrorist incidents	12 (5)	10 (4)	13 (7)
Following 9/11, established new mutual aid agreements for terrorist incidents	11 (6)	3[a] (2)	13 (7)

Standard error of the estimate shown in parentheses. [a]Comparison between agencies that had received funding versus those that has not received funding on variable of interest is statistically significant at 0.10 level. [b]Statistically significant at 0.05 level. [c]Includes CBR, conventional explosives, cyberterrorism, or agroterrorism.

enforcement agencies that had received funding following 9/11 also increased departmental spending on terrorism preparedness, compared to 20 percent of local agencies that had not received funding. The difference between these two groups is more striking when considering reallocation of resources. Sixty-six percent of local agencies that had received funding also internally reallocated resources to focus on terrorism preparedness, as compared to only 9 percent of local agencies that had not received funding.

There were two exceptions to this pattern: updating (or newly establishing) mutual aid agreements and undertaking risk or threat assessments. The last two rows of Table 5.5 show the results for mutual aid agreements. Following 9/11, 12 percent of local law enforcement agencies overall updated existing mutual aid agreements to address terrorist-related incidents.[4] We found no difference between law enforcement agencies who had received funding versus those that had not received funding in the updating of agreements. However, there was a statistically significant difference between agencies with respect to newly establishing mutual aid agreements following 9/11. Here, the pattern is the reverse of what one might expect; while only 3 percent of agencies that had received funding established new mutual aid agreements, 13 percent of law enforcement agencies that had not received any external funding or support did so. Although seemingly anomalous, it may be that these law enforcement agencies were also less likely to have mutual aid agreements to begin with and were trying to catch up after 9/11.

The other exception was with respect to assessment activities. Most local law enforcement agencies (73 percent) had conducted a risk or threat assessment between 2000 and 2002, with the majority of these assessments taking place after 9/11 (Table 5.6). The difference in when the assessments were conducted was mostly the result of an increase in assessment activities (from 19 percent to 54 percent) among the subsample of law enforcement agencies that had not received external funding or support. In Chapters Three and Four, we reported that following 9/11, law enforcement agencies in smaller counties worked to catch up in their assessment activities; however, size of jurisdiction did not appear to be related to receipt of funding. So it is unclear what may be driving this result. However, it suggests that these agencies may differ qualitatively in some important ways (e.g., by size of department) not captured by the above comparison.

Lastly, how high a priority law enforcement agencies assigned to terrorism preparedness appears to be related to receipt of funding. That is, law enforcement agencies who received an increase in funding fol-

---

[4] Overall, 93 percent (S.E. 4) of law enforcement agencies (not shown) have mutual-aid agreements for emergencies in general, with only 1 percent (S.E. 0.06) of agencies' mutual-aid agreements addressing terrorism incidents specifically.

Table 5.6
Relationship Between Receipt of External Funding or Support and Assessment Activities

Conducted Assessment?	All Local LE Orgs. (%)	Local LE Orgs. That Received Funding or Other Support (%)	Local LE Orgs. That Did Not Receive Funding or Other Support (%)
Yes, within past 2 years	73 (8)	71 (14)	74 (10)
Prior to 9/11	23 (8)	40 (14)	19 (9)
After 9/11	52 (11)	42 (14)	54 (13)

Standard error of the estimate shown in parentheses. The assessment variable omits those few cases that indicated they conducted an assessment both before and after 9/11.
The chi-square test that jointly tested for difference between the assessment variable was statistically significant at $p = 0.05$ (Chisq = 7.94 with 3 degrees of freedom).

Table 5.7
Relationship Between Receipt of External Funding or Support and Priority Assigned to Spending Departmental Resources on Terrorism Preparedeness

Priority Rating	All Local LE Orgs. (%)	Local LE Orgs. That Received Funding or Other Support (%)	Local LE Orgs. That Did Not Receive Funding or Other Support (%)
High priority	7 (3)	71 (14)	74 (10)
Somewhat of a priority	21 (6)	42 (13)	16 (6)
Low priority	37 (10)	50 (14)	34 (11)
Not at all a priority	35 (13)	0	44 (15)

Standard error of the estimate shown in parentheses.
The chi-square test that jointly tested for differences between the priority variables was statistically significant at $p < 0.001$ (Chisq = 3028.22 with 3 degrees of freedom).

lowing 9/11 were more likely than other agencies to assign a higher priority to spending departmental resources on terrorism preparedness (Table 5.7). For example, few local law enforcement agencies overall (7 percent) indicated it was a high priority to spend departmental resources on terrorism preparedness, with no difference in rating b1etween those agencies that had received an increase in funding or support versus those that had not. However, we did find significant differences for the other priority ratings. Forty-two percent of local law enforcement agencies that had received an increase in funding or support rated spending departmental resources on terrorism preparedness as being somewhat of a priority, compared to only 16 percent of agencies that had not received an increase. Further, only local law enforcement agencies that had not received an increase in funding said it was not at all a priority for their department to spend resources in this area.

Those Agencies That Assessed the Risk of a Terrorist Attack to Be Higher for Their Jurisdiction Were More Likely to Undertake Preparedness Activities Following 9/11

Table 5.8 shows the distribution of responses for the preparedness indicators we analyzed by level of perceived risk. The three columns (low, medium, high) under "Level of Perceived Risk" indicate what percentage of law enforcement agencies in each of the risk categories undertook a particular preparedness activity.

Law enforcement agencies that perceived the risk of a future terrorist attack to be higher for their jurisdiction were more likely than other agencies following 9/11 to have (1) updated their response plans or SOPs to address terrorism-related incidents, (2) updated their mutual aid agreements to address terrorism-related incidents, (3) conducted or participated in joint training exercises with terrorism-related task forces, and (4) internally reallocated departmental resources to focus on improving response capabilities and preparedness for terrorism-related incidents. Law enforcement agencies that perceived the risk to be higher were also more proactive in conducting risk or threat assessments before 9/11 and tended to assign a higher priority to investing departmental resources on terrorism preparedness (Tables 5.8 and 5.9).

For example, only 9 percent of law enforcement agencies that assessed the risk of a future terrorist attack to be low updated their response plans or SOPs following 9/11, compared to 19 percent of agencies in the medium-risk category and 56 percent of agencies in the high-risk category (Table 5.8). Although not statistically significant, we saw a similar trend for updating mutual aid agreements and increasing departmental spending following 9/11 to improve response capabilities for terrorism.

Law enforcement agencies that perceived the risk to be higher for their jurisdiction, in general, were more likely to have conducted risk

Table 5.8
Relationship Between Perceived Risk and Selected Preparedness Activities, All Local Law Enforcement Organizations (%)

	Level of Perceived Risk			Chi Sq Test of
Preparedness Activities	Low	Medium	High	Stat. Sign.[a]
Yes, department conducted assessment between 2000–2002	56 (24)	83 (11)	85 (8)	NS
Yes, conducted assessment prior to 9/11	3 (3)	40 (17)	31 (10)	NS
Conducted assessment after 9/11	54 (25)	50 (16)	50 (11)	NS
Following 9/11, updated response plans or SOPS to address terrorism-related incidents[b]	9 (6)	19 (9)	56 (11)	$p = 0.0055$
Following 9/11, updated existing mutual-aid agreements for terrorist incidents	1 (1)	19 (12)	19 (9)	$p = 0.0065$
Following 9/11, established new mutual-aid agreements for terrorist incidents	3 (3)	13 (12)	19 (11)	NS
Following 9/11, has conducted joint training exercises	0	9 (5)	31 (10)	$p < 0.001$
Following 9/11, internally increased spending to focus on terrorism preparedness	15 (11)	31 (14)	34 (10)	NS
Following 9/11, internally reallocated resources to focus on terrorism preparedness	8 (6)	17 (9)	40 (11)	$p < 0.05$

Standard error of the estimate shown in parentheses.

[a]Chi-square tests were conducted for each preparedness activity to joint test for differences between risk groups. We report in the last column the *p* value for each of the chi-square tests performed. The assessment variable omits those few cases that conducted an assessment both before and after 9/11.

[b]Includes CBR, conventional explosives, cyberterrorism, or agroterrorism.

or threat assessments before 9/11, whereas those departments that had assessed the risk to be low for their jurisdiction worked to catch up in their assessment activities following 9/11 (Table 5.8). Specifically, although not statistically significant, we found that law enforcement

Table 5.9
Relationship Between Perceived Risk and Priority Assigned to Spending Resources on Terrorism Preparedness, All Local Law Enforcement Organizations

	Level of Perceived Risk (%)			Chi Sq. Test of
Priority Rating	Low	Medium	High	Stat. Sign.
High priority	0.1 (0.1)	0.4 (0.3)	21 (8)	p < 0.001
Somewhat of a priority	7 (5)	23 (10)	36 (11)	
Low priority	16 (10)	59 (15)	41 (11)	
Not at all a priority	77 (13)	18 (14)	2 (2)	

Standard error of the estimate shown in parentheses.

agencies in the low-risk category were less likely than agencies in the medium- and high-risk categories to have conducted a risk or threat assessment between 2000 and 2002. Breaking this down further, very few law enforcement agencies in the low-risk category (3 percent) had conducted an assessment prior to 9/11, compared to the medium-risk (40 percent) and high-risk (31 percent) groups. However, following 9/11, low-risk departments worked to catch up in doing assessments; as a result, approximately half of law enforcement agencies in each risk category conducted an assessment following 9/11.

The higher the level of perceived risk, the higher a priority it was for a law enforcement agency to spend departmental resources on terrorism preparedness. Table 5.9 shows a positive relationship between level of perceived risk and the priority that agencies assigned to spending departmental resources on terrorism preparedness.[5] Law enforcement agencies that perceived the risk to be high were 200 times more likely than the low-risk category and 52 times more likely than the medium-risk category to assign a high priority to spending departmental resources on terrorism preparedness (Table 5.9). Similarly, 36 percent of law enforcement agencies in the high-risk category, compared to 23 percent of agencies in the medium-risk category and 7 percent of agencies in the low-risk category, rated spending departmental re-

[5] Respondents were asked how high a priority it is for their department to spend resources for emergency preparedness for terrorism or for counterterrorism or antiterrorism purposes, compared to other needs that may be facing their department.

sources on terrorism preparedness as somewhat of a priority. Agencies that perceived the risk as being low were much more likely than the medium-risk or high-risk categories (77 percent, 18 percent, and 2 percent, respectively) to indicate it was not at all a priority of their department to spend resources on terrorism preparedness.

Level of perceived risk, though, does not appear to be closely related to size of jurisdiction. That is, even law enforcement agencies in smaller counties, if they perceived the risk of future terrorist attacks to be higher for their jurisdiction, tended to be proactive in addressing terrorism preparedness. Table 5.10 shows the relationship between our measure of perceived risk and size of jurisdiction. For each level of perceived risk, a similar proportion of agencies was located in large counties. That is, roughly 20 percent of local law enforcement agencies in each of the low, medium, and high-risk categories were located in large metropolitan counties (those with a population of 1 million or more). This finding suggests that our measure of perceived risk is capturing factors important to law enforcement in assessing their jurisdiction's level of risk other than simply population size.

Agencies That Assessed the Risk of Future Terrorist Attacks to Be Higher for Their Jurisdiction Were Also More Likely to Receive External Funding Following 9/11

In the above analyses, we showed that receipt of funding and level of perceived risk were positively associated with preparedness. That is, law enforcement agencies that received external funding following 9/11 and law enforcement agencies that perceived the risk of future terrorist attacks as being higher were more likely to have undertaken steps to

Table 5.10
Relationship Between Measure of Perceived Risk and Size of Jurisdiction, All Local Law Enforcement Organizations

Level of Perceived Risk	Large Counties (%)	Smaller Counties (%)
Low	16	84
Medium	20	80
High	22	78

Table 5.11
Relationship Between Level of Perceived Risk and Receipt of External Funding or Resources Following 9/11

	All Local Law Enforcement Orgs. (%)	
Level of Perceived Risk	**Received External Funding and/or Resources Following 9/11**	**Received External Funding Only Following 9/11**
Low	3 (3)	3 (3)
Medium	26 (12)	20 (11)
High	36 (11)	30 (10)

Standard error of the estimate shown in parentheses.
The chi-square test that jointly tested for differences between the priority variables was statistically at $p = 0.04$ (Chisq = 6.27 with 2 degrees of freedom).

improve their level of preparedness and to view terrorism preparedness as being a high priority than those agencies that did not receive funding or that perceived the risk to be lower for their jurisdiction.

What is the relationship between perception of risk and receipt of funding? Table 5.11 shows the distribution of responses for receipt of external funding or resources from any source by level of perceived risk. The first column indicates the percentage of agencies that received external funding or resources, and the second column indicates the percentage of agencies that received external funding only.

Perceived risk was a strong predictor of receipt of funding. Law enforcement agencies that assessed the risk to be higher for their jurisdiction were more likely than those who assessed the risk to be lower to receive external funding following 9/11. For example, only 3 percent of law enforcement agencies in the low-risk category received external funding or resources following 9/11 from any outside source, as compared to 26 percent in the medium-risk category and 36 percent in the high-risk category (Table 5.11).[6]

Still, only about a third of law enforcement agencies that assessed the risk of a future terrorist attack as high reported receiving external

[6] The difference between the low-risk and medium-risk categories was statistically significant, with a p value of 0.07.

funding or resources from any source following 9/11 to support their preparedness activities (Table 5.11).

Discussion

Receipt of External Funding Following 9/11 Was Predictive of Law Enforcement Undertaking Preparedness Activities

Table 5.12 summarizes which specific preparedness activities were correlated with level of perceived risk, size of jurisdiction, and receipt of funding.

In this chapter, we were able to demonstrate a positive relationship between receipt of funding and preparedness. Law enforcement agencies that received an increase in external funding or resources following 9/11 were more likely than other agencies to have (1) increased spending or internally reallocated resources to focus on terrorism preparedness, (2) updated response plans or SOPs to address terrorist-related incidents (particularly CBR-related), (3) established new mutual aid agreements after 9/11 to address terrorist-related incidents, and (4) conducted joint training exercises after 9/11 (Table 5.12). These law enforcement agencies were also more likely to have specialized terrorism units and to assign a higher priority to expending departmental resources on preparedness for terrorism.

Although receipt of funding was predictive of preparedness activities, only one out of five law enforcement agencies reported having received external funding (or resources) from any source following 9/11 to support their terrorism preparedness activities. The identified associations between receipt of funding and preparedness activities, however, do not necessarily imply a causal relationship. For example, law enforcement agencies that were more actively engaged in preparedness activities to begin with may have been more likely to apply for funding and to be successful in obtaining it.

Table 5.12
Summary of Preparedness Activites by Level of Perceived Risk, Size of Jurisdiction, and Receipt of Funding

Preparedness Activities	Local Law Enforcement Agencies That. . .		
In General, Were More Likely to Have:	**Perceived Risk to be Higher for Their Jurisdiction**	**Were Located in Large Metropolitan Counties**	**Received External Funding Following 9/11**
Specialized terrorism units	√	√	√
Assigned a higher priority to expending departmental resources on terrorism preparedness	√	√	√
Conducted assessments before 9/11	√	√	--
Following 9/11, Were More Likely to Have			
Increased spending or internally reallocated resources to focus on terrorism preparedness	√	√	√
Updated response plans to address terrorist-related incidents	√	--	√
Updated mutual aid agreements to address terrorist-related incidents	√	--	--
Developed new mutual aid agreements to address terrorist-related incidents	--	√	--
Conducted joint training exercises with terrorism-related task forces	√	√	√
Received external funding or resources to support preparedness activities	√	--	N/A

For perceived risk, the comparison group is agencies that perceived the risk to be lower; for size of jurisdiction, the comparison group is agencies located in smaller counties; for receipt of external funding, the comparison group is agencies that did not receive funding.

Level of Risk and Size of Jurisdiction Was Also Predictive of Preparedness Activities, but Risk Is a Better Predictor of Funding

In Chapter Three, we found that size of jurisdiction was predictive of law enforcement agencies undertaking steps to improve their level of preparedness. That is, law enforcement agencies located in large counties tended to be more proactive in addressing terrorism preparedness than those located in smaller counties (Table 5.12). Also, law enforcement agencies in large counties were more likely than other agencies to assess the threat of future terrorist attacks as higher for their jurisdiction and to assign a higher priority to investing departmental resources on preparedness.

In this chapter, we found that perceived risk is also predictive of law enforcement agencies undertaking steps to improve their preparedness for terrorism. Law enforcement agencies that perceived the risk of a future terrorist attack to be higher for their jurisdiction were more likely than other agencies to have (1) updated their response plans or SOPs to address terrorism-related incidents, (2) updated their mutual aid agreements to address terrorism-related incidents, (3) conducted or participated in joint training exercises with terrorism-related task forces, and (4) internally reallocated departmental resources to focus on improving response capabilities and preparedness for terrorism-related incidents following 9/11. These agencies also tended to assign a higher priority to investing departmental resources on terrorism preparedness and to be proactive in conducting assessments even before 9/11 (Table 5.12).

Although risk was predictive of receipt of funding, only about a third of law enforcement agencies that assessed the risk to be high for their jurisdiction reported having received external funding (or resources) from any source following 9/11.

At the beginning of this chapter, we were interested in understanding better the relationship between perceived risk, size of jurisdiction, receipt of funding, and preparedness activities. Figure 5.3 summarizes the identified relationships between these indicators.

Although size of jurisdiction and level of perceived risk were both predictive of law enforcement undertaking preparedness activities, risk was the better predictor of receipt of funding. That is, law enforcement

Figure 5.3
Identified Relationships Between Perceived Risk, Size of Jurisdiction, Receipt of Funding, and Preparedness Activities

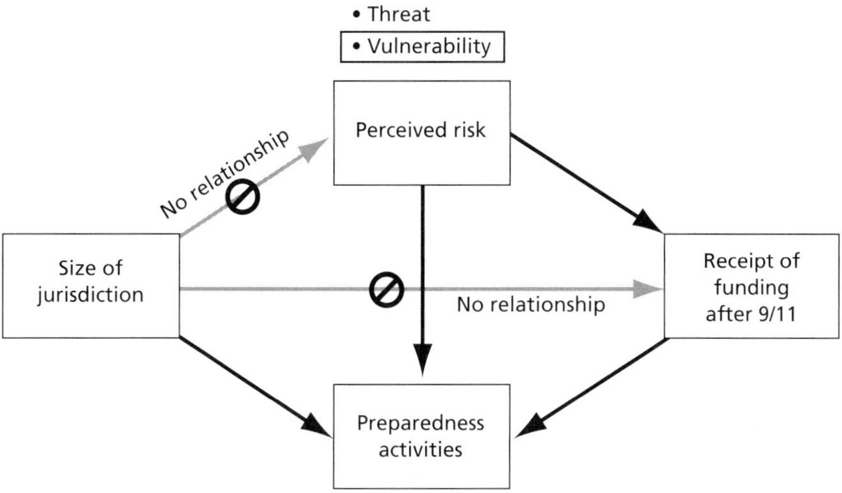

RAND *MG104-5.3*

agencies that assessed the risk to be higher for their jurisdiction tended to receive external funding following 9/11 to support their preparedness activities (Figure 5.3). However, we found little or no relationship between size of jurisdiction and receipt of funding.

The identified association between receipt of funding and level of perceived risk, though, does not necessarily imply a causal relationship. As noted in Chapter Four, soon after 9/11, ODP made available about $800 million in federal funding to the first-responder community. In addition, many state, county, and city governments increased spending on terrorism preparedness following 9/11, with some of that funding going to law enforcement. That is, these results do not necessarily imply that jurisdictions with higher levels of risk were the primary targets of this additional funding. It may have been that law enforcement agencies that perceived the risk of terrorism to be higher for their jurisdiction, in general, were more proactive in seeking funding and more successful at obtaining it.

Homeland-security experts and first responders have cautioned against an overemphasis on improving the preparedness of large cities to the exclusion of smaller communities or rural areas. They note that much of our critical infrastructure and a number of potential high-value targets (nuclear power plants, military installations, agricultural facilities, etc.) are located in less-populated areas, not near large population centers. Importantly, we found no significant relationship between size of jurisdiction and level of perceived risk. That is, perception of risk was not closely correlated with whether an agency was located in a county with a large population. Our results suggest that the story is not simply that law enforcement agencies located in areas with large populations are more proactively engaged in terrorism preparedness than agencies in localities with smaller population sizes. Even law enforcement agencies in smaller counties, if they assessed their risk to be somewhat higher, tended to be proactive in improving their level of preparedness. The fact that both perceived risk and size of jurisdiction were predictive of undertaking preparedness activities but were not strongly correlated with one another suggests that law enforcement agencies were taking both factors into account.

Lastly, we were able to demonstrate that risk perceptions are correlated with the preparedness behavior of law enforcement. What appears to be primarily driving our measure of perceived risk is the vulnerability component of risk versus the threat component, since we found no relationship between size of jurisdiction and level of perceived risk, yet size of jurisdiction was correlated with threat perception. In other words, law enforcement agencies located in jurisdictions with more physical vulnerabilities tend to assign a higher priority to investing departmental resources in preparedness, to be more proactive in improving preparedness, and to be more successful in obtaining external funding support than those law enforcement agencies located in jurisdictions with fewer types of physical vulnerabilities.

CHAPTER SIX

Conclusions and Future Directions

Introduction

Law enforcement has played and will continue to play a critical role in responding to, preventing, and deterring terrorist attacks in the United States. And, as noted in Chapter One, within DHS, ODP is charged with coordinating preparedness efforts and with working with state and local first responders, such as law enforcement, to improve terrorism preparedness, including training, exercises, and equipment support. In addition, ODP is responsible for directing terrorism preparedness grant programs at the federal level for all emergency response providers and for measuring programmatic performance and improvements in domestic preparedness.

Our survey of law enforcement agencies has yielded findings across a number of areas of importance to DHS and ODP as they carry out their mandate: (1) law enforcement's threat perceptions; (2) what law enforcement is doing to counter the threat and shore up vulnerabilities including variation in their approach to preparedness; (3) law enforcement's views about their support needs and what gaps remain; (4) how law enforcement is resourcing its preparedness activities, and the relationship between risk, size of jurisdiction, funding, and preparedness; and (5) law enforcement's evolving intelligence function.

This chapter focuses on the key conclusions and implications for DHS and ODP of those conclusions; we also briefly examine what could be done in the future to make the existing survey even more useful.

Conclusions and Implications

We identify the following eight broad conclusions and discuss them below, along with their implications for DHS and ODP.

Law Enforcement Considers the Most Likely Threats to Be Chemical, Biological, or Conventional-Explosives Attacks

Law enforcement's threat perceptions provide information to DHS and ODP about what types of threats these agencies view as being important to be preparing for. Although about half of local law enforcement agencies assessed the chance of a major terrorist incident occurring within their jurisdiction within the next five years to be very low, one out of five considered the chance of an attack to be somewhat likely or very likely. Law enforcement agencies in large counties, in particular, rated the likelihood of terrorist attacks occurring as relatively high for their jurisdiction. The types of threats local law enforcement was most concerned about were the use of chemical or biological agents or conventional explosives. In addition, they assessed the chance of cyberterrorism occurring to be somewhat likely or very likely. The majority of state law enforcement agencies also viewed the threat of terrorism as being relatively high.

Consistent with their higher threat perceptions, a majority of state law enforcement agencies and local law enforcement agencies within large counties desired better intelligence information from DHS and DOJ about the threat facing their region or jurisdiction to help strengthen their response capabilities and inform assessment activities.

In 2002, the Joint Terrorism Task Forces Were a Key Source of Counterterrorism Training at the Local Level

In terms of training, the JTTFs appear to be a key source of counterterrorism training at the local level, particularly for those law enforcement agencies located within large counties. Most law enforcement agencies in large counties and about a quarter of those in smaller counties reported having interacted with the JTTFs, primarily to receive counterterrorism training. We also found relatively modest levels of reported participation in federally sponsored training programs by local law enforcement. In contrast, few state law enforcement agencies reported receiving counterterrorism training from the JTTFs; instead, they reported greater participation in federally sponsored training programs, suggesting that the JTTFs were not an important source of training for state-level organizations.

Given the increased number of training courses being offered since 9/11, the degree of reliance on the JTTFs for counterterrorism training may lessen over time as more and more local law enforcement participate in other training opportunities. For example, DOJ recently created the portal Web site "Counter-Terrorism Training and Resources for Law Enforcement" to serve as a central source of information on counterterrorism-training resources and opportunities. Then again, the JTTFs may continue to be an important source of awareness training at the local level. We did not ask how extensive that training was, nor what factors, if any, limited local law enforcement's ability to participate in counterterrorism training. However, from other studies, we know that lack of training dollars and funding to pay for overtime or to backfill personnel are key impediments.[1] For local law enforcement, the JTTFs may represent a relatively more affordable option than other training opportunities.

DHS and ODP will want to further consider how to encourage local law enforcement's greater participation in counterterrorism training. One option may be to provide more training resources to the JTTFs. Then again, given the increased demands placed on these task forces since 9/11, it may be difficult for them to take on additional training responsibilities.

Agencies with Specialized Terrorism Units Are More Proactive in Doing Joint Training

Law enforcement agencies with specialized terrorism units, in general, were more proactive in doing joint training. For example, following 9/11 most of these specialized terrorism units at the local level con-

---

[1] L. Davis, L. Mariano, J. Pace, S. Cotton, and P. Steinberg, "Summary of Selected Survey Results," Appendix D, in *Fifth Annual Report to the President and the Congress: Forging America's New Normalcy: Securing Our Homeland, Protecting Our Liberty, by the Advisory Panel to Assess Domestic Response Capabilities for Terrorism Involving Weapons of Mass Destruction,* December 15, 2003.

ducted joint training with other city or county agencies or departments, and about a third participated in joint training with state agencies or the FBI. At the state level, about three-quarters of the specialized terrorism units participated in joint training with other state agencies, and about half with the FBI.

Although the majority of state law enforcement agencies have specialized terrorism units, only a quarter of law enforcement agencies in large counties have established such units.[2] Thus, DHS may want to direct training funds to these specialized units and support the formation of these units at the local level. Given that law enforcement agencies that lacked specialized terrorism units, in general, tended to be less actively engaged in training activities, DHS and ODP also may want to give special attention to engaging more of these law enforcement agencies in training activities.

There Is Variation in Law Enforcement's Approach to Preparedness

The survey results showed variation in law enforcement's approach to preparedness. In general, state law enforcement agencies and local law enforcement agencies were more proactively engaged in terrorism preparedness activities along its different dimensions (planning, training, equipping, coordinating, etc.) than were law enforcement agencies in smaller counties. These findings are consistent with the higher threat perceptions of these agencies and the higher priority that they assigned to investing departmental resources on terrorism preparedness. In addition, at the state level and in large counties, law enforcement appears to play a more central role in terms of planning, training, and assessment activities. For example, state law enforcement agencies and local law enforcement agencies within large counties tend to be responsible for developing contingency plans and conducting assessments for their region and jurisdiction. As discussed

---

[2] The primary responsibilities of these specialized terrorism units at the state and local levels were to liaise with other law enforcement agencies and to assist with intelligence gathering. In addition, those units of state law enforcement and local law enforcement within large counties tended to also be involved in training of other law enforcement personnel, assisting with investigations, and analyzing and disseminating intelligence information.

further below, these agencies also tend to have greater (and a wider range of) support needs.

In comparison, law enforcement agencies in smaller counties tend to be less proactively engaged in addressing terrorism preparedness. Consistent with their lower threat perceptions, these agencies were less likely to have made organizational changes to improve their terrorism response capabilities, such as establishing specialized terrorism units or increasing the number of personnel assigned to do planning. These agencies also had less experience in responding to and investigating terrorist-related incidents and in coordinating with the FBI and other federal agencies. Law enforcement agencies in smaller counties were also less likely to view communications interoperability as a problem for their jurisdiction and, in general, had fewer support needs, as discussed further in the next section.

In smaller counties, interagency task forces appear to play a more important role in terms of planning, assessment, and training activities, suggesting that these task forces are candidates for preparedness funding and training resources. For example, responsibility for developing contingency plans for terrorism at the state level and in large counties rested primarily with law enforcement, whereas in smaller counties interagency task forces also shared this responsibility.

In terms of assessment activities, even before 9/11 many state law enforcement agencies and local law enforcement agencies within large counties had been proactive in doing risk or threat assessments. Assessment activities at the state level and within large counties tended to be more comprehensive and to be primarily the responsibility of law enforcement. In comparison, law enforcement agencies in smaller counties were less proactive in doing assessments before 9/11. Assessment activities in these counties tended to be narrower in scope (focusing mostly on public buildings and key infrastructure) and also to be the responsibility of an interagency task force.

This variation suggests that future programmatic support at the federal, state, and local levels will need to be tailored to take into account these differences. In addition, any initiative to model or develop objective measures of overall U.S. preparedness for terrorism also will need to take this variation into account.

There Is Variation in Law Enforcement's Support Needs

State and local law enforcement also varied in their support needs to conduct future risk or threat assessments and to strengthen response capabilities. DHS and ODP will want to tailor their programmatic approach to providing support in these areas to take into account this variability in support needs.

The Need for Support to Do Assessments. Most state and local law enforcement agencies expressed a desire for some type of support to help them conduct future assessments. However, what they considered to be their most important support need in this area differed. Nearly half of state law enforcement agencies and a third of local law enforcement agencies in large counties desired better intelligence information about the terrorist threat or capability, consistent with their higher threat perceptions. In comparison, few law enforcement agencies located in smaller counties desired this type of support. Instead, many agencies in smaller counties considered protocols for conducting or evaluating assessments as being their most important support need, as did a third of state law enforcement agencies.

Training on how to conduct assessments was the most important support need for a third of local law enforcement agencies (in both large and small counties). However, none of the state law enforcement agencies surveyed listed training as an important support need for doing future assessments, perhaps reflecting the fact that responsibility for doing such assessments tends to fall primarily on localities, with state government's role being more to "roll up" local assessment results into a statewide assessment.

The Need for Support to Strengthen Response Capabilities. The type of support needed to strengthen response capabilities fell into three broad categories: training, equipment, and other types of support. In general, state law enforcement agencies and local law enforcement agencies in large counties tended to have a greater number of support needs, consistent with their higher threat perceptions and their more proactive engagement in preparedness activities. In comparison, law enforcement agencies in smaller counties tended to have fewer support needs, again consistent with their lower threat perceptions and less active engagement in preparedness activities.

To improve response capabilities, training was a particularly important support need for state law enforcement agencies and local law enforcement agencies located within large counties, particularly in the areas of conducting joint operations, conducting tabletop or field exercises, operating in hazardous environments, doing evidence collection, and using the incident command system.

With respect to equipment needs, about half of state and local law enforcement agencies desired support to purchase Levels A or B PPE for their response personnel and training on its usage. Consistent with their desire for training on how to operate in hazardous environments and for more and better PPE, about a third of local law enforcement and two-thirds of state law enforcement agencies also wanted better sensor technology to rapidly identify hazards that their response personnel may encounter.

Manpower shortfalls appeared to be more acute at the state level. The majority of state law enforcement agencies indicated a need for more manpower to enable them to dedicate personnel to response planning and/or counterterrorism activities, as compared to only about a third of local law enforcement agencies.

The Need to Provide Greater Awareness Training. We identified three areas for awareness training that DHS may want to address. The first area is the use of PPE.[3] The survey results suggested an incomplete understanding by law enforcement about the purpose of the different levels of PPE and how they relate to the mission(s) of law enforcement in a hazardous environment situation.

Of the four levels of protective clothing ensembles to be worn when dealing with hazardous materials, Level A PPE provides the greatest level of protection and is intended for those personnel that

---

[3] The ODP, as an entity of DOJ under OJP prior to the creation of DHS, administered the 2001 equipment grant program. These were direct grants (not reimbursement) for planning, training, equipment, and exercises. Many of the initial orders for PPE occurred as part of the Fiscal Year 2001 Equipment grant program process.

must operate in a "hot" zone.[4] Level B PPE is appropriate for conducting a force protection mission in a "warm" zone, whereas Level C PPE provides the least amount of protection and is more suitable for law enforcement personnel at the outer perimeter. Typically, HAZMAT units or personnel from the fire department or from the emergency medical services (EMS) community will be required to operate in a HAZMAT environment. Only a limited number of law enforcement and other agencies' personnel would have to operate in a "hot" zone and thus require Level A PPE. Further, all levels of PPE have a limit on the length of time an individual can safely operate in the protective ensemble, and it would be rare for all on-duty law enforcement staff to require this type of protection.

However, the fact that so many state and local law enforcement agencies indicated a desire for Levels A and B PPE, in particular, suggests either an incomplete understanding of the appropriate use of this equipment as it relates to their mission or possible problems with equipment grant-distribution mechanisms. Specifically, first-responder grant and funding timelines, in some instances, have been compressed, with local law enforcement given short turnaround times to apply for federal funds being distributed through their state governments. Anecdotal evidence suggests that this has resulted in a rush to purchase equipment without adequate time, in some cases, for individual departments to assess their equipment needs.

The second area is awareness of what counterterrorism training is being offered at the local and state levels. Local law enforcement agencies varied in their awareness of what counterterrorism training was being offered by their police academy or by their state government. Somewhat unsettling was the result that about one-third of local law enforcement reported they did not know whether their police academy offered such training. Although about two-thirds of state law enforcement agencies indicated that counterterrorism training was offered by their state, only one out of five local law enforcement agencies were

[4] T. LaTourrette, D. J. Peterson, J. T. Bartis, and B. A. Jackson, *Protecting Emergency Responders*, Vol. 2: *Community Views of Safety and Health Risks and Personal Protection Needs,* Santa Monica, Calif.: RAND Corporation, MR-1646-NIOSH, 2003.

aware of those training opportunities. Law enforcement agencies located in smaller counties, in particular, were unaware of what type of counterterrorism training was being offered at the state level.

The third area of concern is responsibility for developing terrorism contingency plans for a jurisdiction or state. Fifteen percent of local law enforcement respondents did not know who was responsible for developing such plans for their jurisdiction; 3 percent of state law enforcement agencies were uncertain who had this responsibility at the state level.

The Need to Improve Communications Interoperability. As was true in earlier terrorist incidents, the 9/11 attacks highlighted a number of interoperability problems between first responders involved in multiagency response. Many of these problems have been long-standing. For example, in a 1997 survey of wireless communications sponsored by the National Institute of Justice (NIJ) among state and local law enforcement agencies, the two biggest obstacles to interoperability cited were limitations in funding and frequency incompatibility.[5] Other obstacles cited were inadequate systems planning, differences in coverage areas, use of different communication modes (analog versus digital), and institutional factors.[6] At the time of the 1997 NIJ-sponsored survey, many state and local law enforcement agencies expected their interoperability situation to improve, with more than half indicating that their department planned to replace or upgrade their radio systems within the next ten years.

Five years later (and one year following the 9/11 attacks), RAND's 2002 survey results indicate that many state and local law enforcement agencies continue to have interoperability problems, with two factors—lack of funding and aging communications and hardware—being important obstacles to improving interoperability. The majority of state law enforcement agencies and local law enforcement agencies within large counties, in particular, indicated a need to replace aging communications systems and to improve communications interoper-

---

[5] M. J. Taylor, R. C. Epper, and T. K. Tolman, "Wireless Communications and Interoperability among State and Local Law Enforcement Agencies," *National Institute of Justice Research in Brief*, Washington, D.C.: U.S. Department of Justice, Office of Justice Programs, National Institute of Justice, January 1998.

[6] Taylor, Epper, and Tolman, January 1998.

ability. In addition, 24 percent of state law enforcement agencies and 15 percent of law enforcement agencies in large counties—that is, those agencies who assess the threat to be greater—cited differences in resource priorities between emergency response agencies as hindering progress in improving interoperability.

These results suggest that coordinating system planning and acquisition initiatives between multiple response organizations, particularly within the large counties and at the state level, will be important for DHS to focus on. Also, as states and local jurisdictions move forward with replacing aging communications systems and addressing barriers to interoperability, it will be important for DHS to monitor the degree to which detailed guidance on the future technology requirements for public safety communications systems and for interoperability recently put forth by DHS are being adhered to.[7]

Resourcing of Preparedness Raises Concerns about What Trade-Offs May Be Being Made at the Local Level

For many local law enforcement agencies, investing departmental resources on terrorism preparedness was a low priority, compared to other needs of their department. Although not a high priority, about a quarter of local law enforcement agencies increased departmental spending or internally reallocated resources after 9/11 to focus on terrorism preparedness. Law enforcement agencies in large counties, in particular, were more likely to have done so. In addition, those local law enforcement agencies that received an increase in external funding or resources following 9/11 were more likely than other agencies to have (1) increased spending or internally reallocated resources to focus on terrorism preparedness, (2) updated response plans or SOPs to address terrorist-related incidents (particularly CBR-related), (3) established new mutual aid agreements after 9/11 to address terrorist-related incidents, and (4) conducted joint training exercises after 9/11. Although receipt of funding was predictive of undertaking preparedness activities, only one out of five law enforce-

---

[7] In May 2004, DHS announced the release of a wireless-communications plan that provided detailed guidance on the future technology requirements for public-safety communications systems and interoperability. DHS, "Homeland Security First to Define Interoperability Requirements for Nation's First Responder Community," Washington, D.C., April 26, 2004.

ment agencies (in large and small counties) reported receiving external funding (or resources) from any source following 9/11 to support their terrorism preparedness activities.

These survey results, importantly, raise the question of what perhaps was not getting done at the local level following 9/11. That is, what sort of public safety activities may have been sacrificed as a result of shifting of resources or personnel to focus on terrorism preparedness and response? One can make the argument that emergency preparedness for terrorism may go hand in hand with law enforcement's other public safety duties. Thus, it may be that nothing in the system gave. Yet these results suggest that in taking on these additional demands, some local departments may have been stretched thin during that first year after 9/11.

Soon after 9/11, ODP made available about $800 million in federal preparedness funding to the first-responder community. In addition, many state and local city and county governments increased spending on terrorism preparedness, with some of that funding going to law enforcement. By the time of our survey in fall 2002, it may have been that only a portion of this funding had been distributed to local law enforcement. Although more local law enforcement agencies may have received external funding since 2002 to support preparedness activities, the evidence suggests that the receipt and spending of federal first-responder grant funds has been slow.[8] Further, the nation's renewed focus on improving domestic preparedness for terrorism has come at a time when many state, county, and city governments are experiencing severe fiscal crises.

As a result, investments in terrorism preparedness have had to compete with other state and local priorities. Given economic conditions at the local and state levels and delays in the distribution and spending of federal first-responder grant funds, the question of what other public

---

[8] A recent report on the distribution and spending of ODP first-responder grant funds by the DHS Security Inspector General's Office found that the receipt and spending of these funds has been slow. For example, as of February 2004, the majority of the $882 million in the FY 2002 SDPP and FY 2003 SHSGP first-responder grant funds awarded by ODP still remained in the U.S. Treasury. By February 2004, of the $316 million in FY 2002 SDPP funds awarded, only 36 percent of awards had been drawn down. DHS, Office of the Inspector General, "An Audit of Distributing and Spending 'First-Responder' Grant Funds," Report No. OIG-04-15, March 2004.

safety duties may being sacrificed at the local level to meet increased homeland-security demands remains a valid concern. DHS will want to monitor and assess the degree to which this may be the case as first-responder funding begins to reach more and more localities.

Perceived Risk Is Predictive of Law Enforcement Undertaking Steps to Improve Their Preparedness and of Receipt of Funding

Perception of risk was found to be predictive of law enforcement taking steps to improve their level of preparedness for terrorism. Those law enforcement agencies that perceived the risk of a future terrorist attack to be higher for their jurisdiction were more likely than other agencies to have (1) updated their response plans or SOPs and mutual aid agreements to address terrorism-related incidents, (2) conducted or participated in joint training exercises with terrorism-related task forces, and (3) internally reallocated departmental resources to focus on improving response capabilities and preparedness for terrorism-related incidents following 9/11. These agencies also tended to assign a higher priority to investing departmental resources on terrorism preparedness and to be proactive in conducting assessments even before 9/11. What appeared to be driving our measure of perceived risk was primarily the vulnerability component versus the threat component of risk.[9]

Perception of risk also was predictive of receipt of funding. That is, law enforcement agencies that assessed the risk to be higher for their jurisdiction were more likely to receive external funding following 9/11 than those that assessed the risk of terrorism to be lower. However, the identified associations between level of risk and receipt of funding (and receipt of funding and preparedness activities) do not necessarily imply causal relationships. It may be that law enforcement agencies that perceived the risk of terrorism to be higher for their jurisdiction, in general, were more proactive in seeking funding and more successful at obtaining it. Similarly, law enforcement agencies that were more actively engaged in preparedness activities to begin with also may have been more likely to apply for funding following 9/11.

---

[9] We found no relationship between size of jurisdiction and level of perceived risk, yet size of jurisdiction was positively correlated with perception of threat.

ODP is interested in the question of whether jurisdictions of different sizes and risk levels should be prepared at the same level. Homeland-security experts and first responders have cautioned against an overemphasis on improving the preparedness of large cities to the exclusion of smaller communities or rural areas, noting that much of our critical infrastructure and some potential high-value targets (nuclear power plants, military installations, agricultural facilities, etc.) are located in less-populated areas. Importantly, we found that perception of risk was not correlated with size of jurisdiction. That is, even law enforcement agencies in smaller counties, if they assessed the risk to be higher for their jurisdiction, were proactive in improving their level of preparedness. The fact that both perceived risk and size of jurisdiction were predictive of undertaking preparedness activities, but were not strongly correlated with one another, suggests that law enforcement agencies are taking both factors into account.

A criticism of the statewide assessment process has been that in the past the formula for distributing first-responder grant funds has not taken into account differences in threat levels between localities. The 2003 statewide assessment process conducted by DHS was intended to gather information on differences in threat levels to help guide future resource-allocation decisions. Towards this end, state and local organizations were asked to conduct threat and vulnerability assessments, as well as assessments of capabilities and needs, to serve as inputs into the statewide Homeland Security Strategy. The timeline for completing the assessments was compressed, and there were reported inconsistencies across the states in how the assessments were conducted.

Our measures of perceived risk and perceived threat could be used to help validate those assessments. Comparing and correlating the objective measures of threat and vulnerability collected as part of the statewide assessment process with our measures of perceived risk and threat would be a fruitful area for future analysis. Specifically, it would allow DHS to examine the relationship between objective measures of vulnerability and risk obtained through the statewide assessments, subjective assessments of risk, and how these measures correlate with first-responders' preparedness activities and support needs.

Law Enforcement's Intelligence Role is Evolving

In the aftermath of the 9/11 attacks, federal, state, and local law enforcement agencies have recognized "the need to develop new capabilities and methods of deterring crime and terrorist activities."[10] We found that since the 9/11 attacks, law enforcement agencies (particularly those in large counties and at the state level) have organized themselves to expand their intelligence function; this includes assigning personnel to liaise with state-level or city- and county-level interagency task forces and creating specialized units or other structures to focus on counterterrorism. Nearly all state law enforcement agencies had interacted with the FBI's JTTFs, primarily to share intelligence information or to assist with investigations. In addition, many local law enforcement agencies, particularly those in large counties, had interacted with the JTTFs for the purpose of sharing intelligence information and/or counterterrorism training. Overall, two-thirds of local law enforcement—and nearly three-quarters of state law enforcement—agencies received guidance from the FBI following 9/11 as to what type of information to collect and pass on.

Still, one out of five local law enforcement agencies and nearly half of state law enforcement organizations surveyed indicated a need for better intelligence on the terrorist threat and terrorist capability. In written comments received from survey respondents, 17 law enforcement agencies identified the intelligence area (specifically, inadequate intelligence information on the threat, lack of coordination with federal agencies, and lack of trained staff on criminal intelligence) as one of the three most critical areas where their department was the weakest.

Effective sharing of intelligence information between the federal, state, and local levels, however, requires overcoming a number of organizational and institutional barriers. One important impediment has been the lack of integrated information systems to promote information sharing across all levels of government.[11] A GAO study found that federal, state, and city officials generally did not consider the cur-

[10] Office of Justice Programs, U.S. Department of Justice, The National Criminal Intelligence Sharing Plan, Version 1.0, October, 2003, p. iii.

[11] GAO, "Homeland Security: Efforts to Improve Information Sharing Need to be Strengthened," Report No. GAO-03-760, August 2003; Office of Justice Programs, U.S. Department of Justice, October 2003.

rent process for sharing terrorism-related information to be effective. Federal, state, and local officials interviewed or surveyed by the GAO identified three major systemic problems: (1) no level of government was satisfied that they had received enough information; (2) no level of government was satisfied with the timeliness, accuracy, or relevance of the information received; and (3) the federal government still perceives the fight against terrorism, particularly prevention, as primarily a federal responsibility.[12]

A number of initiatives are now underway to enhance information sharing and coordination on intelligence issues. At the grassroots level, ODP and DHS have recently funded the UASI program, whose aim is to increase the security and preparedness of our urban areas.[13] As part of this effort, the UASI program is supporting the development of local, multijurisdictional, multidisciplinary Urban Area Working Groups (UAWGs) that will be responsible for coordinating preparedness activities for their area, conducting urban area assessments and capabilities and needs assessments, and developing security strategies for their urban areas. ODP is offering UASI program participants training and technical assistance to establish interagency working groups modeled after Los Angeles County's Terrorism Early Warning Group (TEWG) in order to improve local capabilities for analyzing strategic and operational information.

At the information-technology level, DHS is in the process of developing a blueprint for the national enterprise architecture for homeland security. Under the direction of the CIA, the Terrorist Threat Integration Center (TTIC) has been established with the aim of centralizing information from all sources on the terrorist threat so that it can be shared, integrated, and analyzed to form a comprehensive picture.[14] In addition, a

---

[12] GAO, August 2003.

[13] The initial participants in this program include 39 urban areas, 20 mass transit systems, and 14 port zones.

[14] For a summary of key initiatives, see the GAO, August 2003. For initiatives undertaken by the FBI, see DOJ, Office of the Inspector General, *The Federal Bureau of Investigation's Efforts to Improve the Sharing of Intelligence and Other Information*, Audit Report No. 04-10, December 2003.

working group comprised of representatives from local, state, tribal, and federal law enforcement agencies and organizations recently put forth a National Criminal Intelligence Sharing Plan to serve as a road map so that "effective intelligence sharing becomes institutionalized throughout the law enforcement community nationwide."[15]

Current trends suggest that law enforcement may play an increasingly important role in the investigation of terrorist-related incidents. Although the FBI has been designated as the lead agency on terrorist investigations, the large number of leads coming in from a variety of sources suggests that follow-up investigations may increasingly be conducted by local law enforcement agencies at the request of the FBI, in part because of the sheer volume of cases. Also, in light of the enactment of the USA Patriot Act and other changes made following 9/11, some experts feel that law enforcement may be called upon to act more broadly now to fill the gap between what federal agencies, such as the FBI, are restricted in doing versus what local law enforcement can contribute in terms of intelligence collection. Beginning in the 1960s, the United States witnessed a decrease in the number of law enforcement agencies with criminal-intelligence units, with some agencies dismantling their units in response to lawsuits and judgments about the misapplication of their criminal-intelligence function against individual citizens.[16] One future trend we may see in light of the war on terrorism is an increase over time in the number of law enforcement agencies that have distinct criminal-intelligence (or terrorism) units and/or have expanded their intelligence functions and are providing intelligence training to more of their law enforcement personnel.

Overcoming impediments to information sharing and coordination is important to achieve. At the same time, given the above trends, the role and function of these specialized terrorism or criminal intelligence units and the intelligence training law enforcement personnel receive will be important for DHS and DOJ to monitor.

---

[15] Office of Justice Programs, U.S. Department of Justice, October 2003, p. vi.

[16] Office of Justice Programs, U.S. Department of Justice, October 2003, p. 26.

Future Directions: Getting the Most Out of the Survey

This study has shown that survey data can be used to better understand variation in law enforcement's prior experience with terrorist-related hoaxes or incidents and in their perceptions about the threat and the risk to their jurisdiction or state and how that relates to the preparedness activities they have undertaken since 9/11. These results also informed us about differences in the approaches adopted by law enforcement agencies in smaller and larger jurisdictions to address terrorism preparedness.

In thinking about how to get the most out of the survey in the future, it is important to recognize that because the survey was given when it was, it provides a unique baseline. First, the survey was conducted one year after the 9/11 attacks. As a result, it provides invaluable information about where the law enforcement community and state OEMs stand currently with respect to domestic preparedness, as well as information on law enforcement's response to 9/11. Second, the survey was conducted just prior to the formation of DHS. Thus, these survey results provide DHS and ODP (as well as other federal departments) with a unique way to gauge where the law enforcement community stood on the eve of the formation of DHS and prior to additional federal funding to improve their preparedness for terrorism. It is also informative about how law enforcement is resourcing their preparedness activities and differences in their support needs.

As DHS and other federal departments move forward with key initiatives to address preparedness gaps and to develop performance measures, it will be important to understand how identified variation in law enforcement's approach to preparedness and in their support needs has changed over time. Thus, leveraging off the baseline quality of the survey by repeating a survey like this one on a biannual basis (i.e., making it a longitudinal survey) can provide DHS, ODP, and other federal departments with a way to gauge the progress of their programs in improving domestic preparedness and in meeting programmatic goals for supporting state and local responders, to assess in how current federal preparedness grant programs are making a difference and in what areas there is room for improvement.

At the beginning of Chapter Three, we noted that preparedness is comprised of a number of different elements that any model of U.S. preparedness for terrorism must take into account. Our 2002 survey collected information on a number of these elements; however, if the survey is made longitudinal, new information should be collected in the following areas to gain greater specificity:

- degree to which mutual aid capacities been tested through exercises
- regional coordination mechanisms that exist for sharing resources and for coordinating response mechanisms
- number of personnel who have been trained in terrorism prevention and response and to what level
- number and types of exercises conducted, and how lessons learned from such exercises are incorporated to address identified shortfalls in response plans, policies, and procedures
- type of equipment purchased or acquired and number of personnel trained in its use
- degree to which annual recurring maintenance costs and replacement timetables for equipment have been addressed and degree to which sustainment of training has been addressed
- barriers to participation in federally sponsored training and equipment programs
- progress made in addressing communications interoperability problems
- resources organizations have received to support their preparedness activities, including amount of funding received, from what sources, for what purposes, and how it compares to their total budget, as well as any shortfalls.

Beyond gathering more and more specific information, any follow-up survey should expand beyond the 2002 survey focus on state and local law enforcement to include all first-responder organizations (e.g., fire service, EMS, emergency management); this will enable DHS to gain a comprehensive picture of how first responders are addressing domestic preparedness at the state and local levels and, collectively, what that means in terms of overall U.S. preparedness for terrorism.

In addition, the sampling approach we used in this survey purposely replicated the sampling design implemented in the original 1995 survey, where the aim was to achieve geographic representation as well as variation in terms of size of department and size of county. Future survey efforts might consider a different sampling approach that, for example, stratifies organizations by level of risk.

Finally, as discussed above in this chapter, comparing and correlating the objective measures of risk collected as part of DHS's statewide assessment process with our measure of perceived risk would be a fruitful area for future analysis. Specifically, it will be important to examine the relationship between objective measures of vulnerability and risk obtained through the statewide assessments, and between our measure of perceived risk and these measures' correlation with response organizations' preparedness activities and support needs.

APPENDIX A

Study Methodology

In this appendix, we discuss how we designed the survey, how we constructed the sampling design strategy, how we fielded the survey (along with the response rates), and how we prepared the survey data for analysis (in particular, the weighting scheme used).

Survey Design and Methods

In this section, we discuss the survey format and the pretesting of the survey instrument.

Survey Format

The law enforcement survey instrument contained four sections: (1) threat environment and organizational experience, (2) departmental resources post-9/11, (3) emergency response planning activities, and (4) organizational information. In addition to the sections shown in Table A.1, we included several questions at the end of the survey instrument to collect information on the individual completing the survey; we also provided an opportunity for the respondent to share additional, open-ended comments and suggestions on other issues of importance to their organization that the survey had not addressed.

The survey instruments were designed as a mail survey that would elicit information on the above-listed areas using structured, semistructured, and open-ended questions. For example, for perceptual items, we used Likert-type scales; for questions requesting information on planning activities, we used checklists; and for questions about ways to

Table A.1
Law Enforcement Agencies Survey Outline

Section 1. Threat Environment and Organizational Experience
• Assessed likelihood of major terrorist incidents happening in jurisdiction in next five years
• Experience since 9/11 with terrorist hoaxes or incidents
• Facilities within jurisdiction or region that may be vulnerable to attack
• Information sources used about potential threat to jurisdiction or state
• Risk- and threat-assessment activities since 9/11
• Participation in interagency task forces to address terrorism preparedness
• Coordination activities with other organizations and agencies
Section 2. Departmental Resources Post-9/11
• Changes in spending or reallocation of resources since 9/11 to improve response capabilities
• Receipt of external funding and/or resources to support preparedness activities
• Priority assigned to expending resources on terrorism preparedness compared to other organizational needs
Section 3. Emergency Response Planning Activities
• Organizational participation in emergency-response planning activities and task forces
• Changes made to emergency-response plans or mutual-aid agreements since 9/11
• Joint preparedness activities, including participation on task forces
• Communications interoperability issues
• Training, exercises, and equipping activities
• Equipment acquisition or purchasing since 9/11
• Self-assessed areas of weaknesses and support needs to improve response capabilities
Section 4. Organizational Information
• Organizational characteristics, including type of organization, size of organization, specialized functions, size of jurisdiction, and size of population the department serves

improve coordination between the federal, state, and local levels and the organization's level of preparedness and support needs, we used a combination of the above, along with open-ended items.

Pretesting the Survey Instrument

Once the initial draft instrument was ready, the surveys were reviewed and pretested to refine and test the draft questionnaire. Survey instruments were then revised according to feedback from each reviewer. This process of instrument construction was essential in helping us pinpoint and fix instrument problems, streamline questions, and reduce respondent burden.

Sampling Design

Since we surveyed representatives from each state for the state organizations involved, there were no sampling design issues for the state organizations. We surveyed a census of state law enforcement organizations in each of the 50 states and used a finite population correction to derive the standard errors for these state-level organizations.

Only the local organizations—in this case, the local law enforcement agencies, the targeted law enforcement sample, and harbor and airport police—required a sampling design. Those are described below.

Local Law Enforcement Sample

For the local law enforcement agencies, we used the National Public Information Safety Bureau (NPSIB) database to select our sample. Replicating the methodology used in the 1995 Riley and Hoffman RAND study, we used a two-stage sampling design, first selecting counties and then law enforcement agencies within those counties. Table A.2 shows the results of the three-step process for selecting counties in the first stage. We began by selecting 16 counties we considered important for inclusion in our sample, based on past experience with major terrorist-related incidents or those locations that have hosted or will host major events (e.g., the Olympics) that might have heightened their sensitivity to the threat of terrorism. The most prominent of each type of response organization within each of these counties was then surveyed. We developed the criteria used to select these jurisdictions based on consultation with terrorism experts from RAND and other organizations.

Next, we divided all the counties into the four census regions and selected the 3 largest counties within each region, subject to the constraint that no 2 counties come from the same state and allowing the previously mentioned 16 counties to be considered for selection. The result was the addition of seven more counties.

Table A.2
Results of Three-Step County-Selection Process for Local Law Enforcement Agencies

Step 1: Counties Hypothesized to Have a Heightened Sensitivity to Threat of Terrorism	Step 2: Largest Counties in Four Census Regions	Step 3: Random Sample of Counties by Size[b] and Region
Los Angeles (CA) Cook (IL) King (WA) New York (NY) Dade (FL) Multnomah (OR) Fulton (GA) Oklahoma (OK) Salt Lake (UT) San Francisco (CA) Montgomery (MD) Prince George's (MD) Arlington (VA) Washington, D.C. Bronx (NY) Queens (NY) 16 counties	Region 1: Middlesex (MA); Philadelphia (PA); Queens (NY)[a] Region 2: Wayne (MI); Cuyahoga (OH); Cook (IL)[b] Region 3: Harris (TX); Fairfax (VA); Dade (FL) Region 4: Maricopa (AZ); Los Angeles (CA)[a]; King (WA)[a] 7 additional counties	Region 1: small, medium, and large (9 counties; 3 in each size) Region 2: small, medium, and large (9 counties; 3 in each size) Region 3: small, medium, and large (9 counties; 3 in each size) Region 4: small, medium, and large (9 counties; 3 in each size) 36 additional counties

[a]County already selected in Step 1;
[b] small = <100,000; medium = >100,000-500,000; large = >500,0000

Finally, within each census region, we split the remaining counties into three groups: counties with a population greater than 500,000, counties with a population between 100,000 and 500,000, and counties with a population less than 100,000. Within each region and population category, three counties were randomly sampled. The result was the addition of 36 more counties. In total, there were 59 counties in the sample.

The second stage of sampling was to select local law enforcement agencies within each of the 59 counties to survey. First, we identified for each county the municipal or county law enforcement agency of the county seat and included them in the sample. Then we stratified the remaining law enforcement agencies within the county by departmental size and randomly selected one agency from each of the three strata. We defined small departments as those having fewer than 31 officers, medium as having 31 to 100 officers, and large as having more than 100 officers. In smaller and/or rural counties, we expected that the number of law enforcement agencies would constrain our ability to sample agencies in each of the departmental-size strata. We selected 107 agencies based on the county seat, and 104 agencies were randomly sampled, for a total of 211 local law enforcement agencies.

Targeted Law Enforcement Sample

To select the targeted sample of local law enforcement agencies, our initial plan was to identify local jurisdictions that had experienced a terrorist incident that resulted in an indictment between 1995 and 2003 (as defined by the FBI and inclusion in the National Terrorism Database (NTD). Approximately 50 jurisdictions have experienced terrorist attacks during these years, with some states experiencing multiple incidents.

The FBI files that contained information on indictments from September 1998 to the present were not available to the project leaders in time for us to use this source to complete the drawing of the sample of law enforcement agencies in jurisdictions that had terrorist acts that led to an indictment. Therefore, we were only able to draw for our target sample a law enforcement agency from each of the jurisdictions for which we had data from January 1995 to August 1998. This resulted in a sample of 37 agencies.

Harbor and Airport Police Sample

We also drew a purposeful sample of 29 harbor and airport law enforcement agencies in major metropolitan areas and port cities. To do so, we used the NPSIB database to select our sample, focusing on a cross section of ports of entry. The harbor and airport sample was drawn from the following cities: Phoenix, Arizona; Huntsville, Alabama; Los Angeles, California; Seattle, Washington; San Francisco, California; San Jose, California; San Pedro, California; Colorado Springs, Colorado; Washington, D.C.; Miami, Florida; Chicago, Illinois; Atlanta, Georgia; Indianapolis, Indiana; Kalamazoo, Michigan; Detroit, Michigan; Cleveland, Ohio; Oklahoma City, Oklahoma; Portland, Oregon; Philadelphia, Pennsylvania; Salt Lake City, Utah; Bridgeport, West Virginia; New York, New York; and Raleigh-Durham, North Carolina.

Overview of the Fielding Process

The data-collection process was conducted through a mail survey (with telephone follow-up), with individually crafted questions for each responder population. The primary components involved in fielding the survey were as follows:

- an advance letter from the RAND principal investigator
- the survey packet itself, which contained a cover letter from MIPT, the survey booklet, and a commemorative "Preventing Terrorism" pen used as a response incentive[1]
- telephone follow-up to ensure arrival of the survey and to emphasize the importance of the study
- the establishment of a toll-free 800 number to field respondent questions
- follow-up postcard reminders mailed two weeks after the survey mailing
- the mailing of a second, replacement survey
- the final round of telephone follow-up.

We discuss the components in more detail below.

Data collection for this survey was primarily conducted between September and November 2002. To better manage the fielding process, the three types of organizations were divided into groups, or "waves."

---

[1] F. Fowler, Jr., *Survey Research Methods*, 2nd ed., Newbury Park, Calif.: Sage Publications, 1993.

The data-collection schedule for each was staggered by approximately seven days to allow the telephone-survey staff adequate time to contact each respondent during the various phases of telephone follow-up. Each survey wave opened with an advance letter to the respondent indicating the importance of the survey and alerting them to its imminent arrival. Advance letters were printed on RAND stationary and signed by the RAND principal investigator. Seven days following the advance letter mailing, the survey was sent out with a cover letter and commemorative pen (imprinted with the phrase *Preventing Terrorism*); the cover letter was printed on MIPT stationary and signed by the Dennis Reimer, director of MIPT. The cover letter gave the addressee the option of assigning a knowledgeable survey designee if the addressee deemed it appropriate. The survey itself was bound in a brightly colored cover, which was designed to attract attention once it was removed from its envelope.

Concurrent with the arrival of the survey packet, the first round of telephone follow-up began. RAND Survey Research Group (SRG) telephone interviewers working from a centralized telephone interviewing facility located in RAND's Santa Monica, California, office conducted this wave of calling.[2] In all rounds of telephone follow-up, interviewers spoke either to the person to whom the packet was mailed or, in cases where that was impossible, to that person's assistant or secretary. The purpose of the first round of calling was to verify that the packet had been received, to reiterate the importance of the respondent's participation in the study, and to answer any questions or concerns that the respondent might have. First-round calling continued for approximately seven days for each sample wave.

Ten days following the survey mailing, reminder postcards were sent out to all cases. The postcard thanked respondents if they had

---

[2] Telephone staff received two days of structured training, with an additional two days allowed for unstructured computer-assisted telephone interviewing (CATI) practice before initiating calls. During the training, interviewers were instructed in survey-research methodology, the use of the CATI system, basic tracking methods, refusal conversion techniques, specific details relating to the characteristics of each responder group with which they would be coming in contact, and issues surrounding the study. In addition, interviewers were required to pass a test with a mock respondent before they were allowed to proceed with the calling.

already filled out and returned the survey, but also prodded them to complete the survey if they had not done so already. The importance of the study and their participation in it was again communicated.

Approximately three and a half weeks following the initial mailing of the survey packet, a replacement survey was mailed to all candidates for whom a returned survey was not on file. One week following this second survey mailing, second-round telephone follow-up began, with interviewers stepping up attempts to convert potential survey refusals.

Survey Response Rates

Table A.3 shows the final response rates for the three surveys. Overall, we achieved a high response rate.

Weighting the Sample

Survey weighting was done for the local law enforcement sample and the state departments of agriculture sample. We discuss each below.

Local Law Enforcement Weighting Scheme

Survey weights were calculated to take into account differences in each local law enforcement agency's probability of being selected into the sample and for nonresponse. By weighting each organization during the analysis, we could make inferences about all local law enforcement agencies in the nation. Each organization's survey weight can be expressed as $w_{ijr} = 1 / p_{ijr}$, where p_{ijr} is the probability that agency *i* in county *j* in region *r* was selected and completed the survey. This probability is the product of three parts:

$$
\begin{aligned}
P_{ijr} = {} & P\ (\text{country } j \text{ selected}) \times \\
& P\ (\text{agency } i \text{ selected} \mid \text{county } j \text{ selected}) \times \\
& P\ (\text{agency } i \text{ responded} \mid \text{agency } i \text{ selected})
\end{aligned}
$$

Table A.3
Final Response for the Survey

Response Organizations	Number of Orgs. Surveyed	Number of Orgs. Responding	Response Rate
	Local Organizations		
Local law enforcement	209*	169	81
Targeted law enforcement sample	37	29	78
Harbor and airport law enforcement	29	15	52
	State Organizations		
State law enforcement	50	39	78
Total/overall rate	325	252	78

[a]Two counties were ineligible for inclusion in the survey.

1. the probability that county *j* was selected
2. the probability that agency *i* was selected, given county *j* was selected
3. the probability that agency *i* responded to the survey, given the agency was selected.

The third part accounts for the fact that certain agencies may be more likely to respond to the survey than others. We hypothesized that region, county size, and department size may affect how likely an organization was to respond. The only difference that we observed was that organizations in the West were more likely to respond than organizations in other regions. The response probabilities for each region were Northeast, 0.66; Midwest, 0.72; South, 0.82; and West, 0.85. Therefore, we compute *P*(agency *i* responded | agency *i* selected) as the fraction of surveyed agencies from the same region that responded to the survey.

APPENDIX B

Analysis of Perceived Threat and Characteristics of Law Enforcement Agencies

For the measure of perceived threat that we constructed, we were interested in understanding what characteristics of law enforcement agencies surveyed may affect their threat categorization. To do so, we fitted a logistic regression model to try to distinguish between low-threat agencies and medium/high threat agencies. Our model included indicators for large ("metro") and small ("non-metro") counties, size of department, and census region.

Predictors of Perceived Threat: Logistic Regression Model

svyglm(formula = medhigh.threat ~ METRO + SIZE + CENS.REG, design = design, family = binomial)

Coefficients: Estimate Std. Error t value Pr(>|t|)

(Intercept)	1.3710	0.6867	1.997	0.04759	*
METRO	–0.8532	0.7862	–1.085	0.27948	
SIZE30–100	2.3558	1.2413	1.898	0.05955	.
SIZE100+	2.2098	0.8951	2.469	0.01463	*
CENS.REG2	–0.6895	1.0212	–0.675	0.50053	
CENS.REG3	–2.9101	1.0891	–2.672	0.00834	**
CENS.REG4	–2.2488	1.0531	–2.135	0.03428	*

Signif. codes: 0 '***' 0.001 '**' 0.01 '*' 0.05 '.' 0.1 ' ' 1
Wald test for CENS.REG
Chisq = 7.52 on 3 df: p = 0.06
Wald test for SIZE
Chisq = 6.23 on 2 df: p = 0.04

We found no differences between agencies in metro and non-metro counties. Both department size and census region, however, were predictive of the chance of an agency being in the medium/high threat category. The odds of being in the medium/high threat category was more than nine times higher for law enforcement agencies with more than 30 officers than for agencies with less than 30 officers. There did not appear to be a difference between medium-size agencies (30–100 officers) and large-size agencies (more than 100 officers). After adjusting for metro and non-metro locality and department size, we found that law enforcement agencies in census region 3 (South) and census region 4 (West) were most likely to be in the low-threat category, while the odds of an agency being in the medium/high threat category was nine times higher for agencies in census region 1 (Northeast) and census region 2 (Midwest), with census region 1 reporting the greatest threat.

References

Associated Press, "House Passes $4.6 Billion Bioterror Bill," Fox News, May 22, 2002, http://www.foxnews.com/story/0,2933,53441,00.html.

Cochran, W. G., Chapter 5, *Sampling Techniques*, New York: Wiley, 1977.

Davis, L., L. Mariano, J. Pace, S. Cotton, and P. Steinberg, "Summary of Selected Survey Results," Appendix D, in *Fifth Annual Report to the President and the Congress: Forging America's New Normalcy: Securing Our Homeland, Protecting Our Liberty, by the Advisory Panel to Assess Domestic Response Capabilities for Terrorism Involving Weapons of Mass Destruction*, December 15, 2003.

DHS—*see* U.S. Department of Homeland Security.

DOJ—*see* U.S. Department of Justice.

Falkenrath, R. A., "The Problems of Preparedness: Challenges Facing the U.S. Domestic Preparedness Program," Cambridge, Mass.: John F. Kennedy School of Government, Harvard University, BCSIA Discussion Paper 2000-28, December 2000.

FBI—*see* Federal Bureau of Investigation.

Federal Bureau of Investigation, War on Terrorism: Counterterrorism, http://www.fbi.gov/terrorinfo/counterrorism/partnership.htm (as of December 9, 2003).

Fowler, F., Jr., *Survey Research Methods,* 2nd ed., Newbury Park, Calif., Sage Publications, 1993.

GAO—*see* U.S. General Accounting Office.

Gorman, S., "Homeland Security Chair Calls for Restraint in First Responder Spending," *National Journal,* November 14, 2003. Online at http://www.govexec.com/dailyfed/1103/111403nj1.htm (as of February 5, 2004).

Hirschkorn, P., "9/11 Panel Focuses on Rescue Efforts: Communication Troubles Cited in Response to New York Attacks," CNN, May 18, 2004, http://www.cnn.com/2004/US/05/18/911.commission/ (as of June 4, 2004).

Hoffman B., *Al Qaeda, Trends in Terrorism and Future Potentialities: An Assessment,* Santa Monica, Calif.: RAND Corporation, P-8078, 2003.

LaTourrette, T., D. J. Peterson, J. T. Bartis, and B. A. Jackson, *Protecting Emergency Responders,* Vol. 2: *Community Views of Safety and Health Risks and Personal Protection Needs,* Santa Monica, Calif.: RAND Corporation, MR-1646-NIOSH, 2003.

MIPT—*see* National Memorial Institute for the Prevention of Terrorism.

National League of Cities, "Homeland Security and America's Cities, Research Brief on America's Cities," National League of Cities, December 2002.

National Legislative Services and Security Association, homepage, http://www.ncsl.org/programs/legman/nlssa/sthomelandoffcs.htm (as of January 7, 2004).

The National Memorial Institute for the Prevention of Terrorism, "Terrorism Indictment Database: Researchers Release Terrorism Database to Scholars Nationwide," Oklahoma City, Okla., November 20, 2003. Online at http://www.mipt.org/Terrorism-Indictment-Database.asp (as of January 15, 2003).

Office for State and Local Domestic Preparedness Support, *Fiscal Year 2000 State Domestic Preparedness Equipment Program,* http://www.ojp.usdoj.gov/fundopps.htm (as of June 4, 2004).

———, *Fiscal Year 2001, Nunn-Lugar-Domenici Domestic Preparedness Program: Program Guidelines and Kit,* Washington, D.C.: U.S. Department of Justice, Office of Justice Programs, Office for State and Local Domestic Preparedness Support, 2001.

Office of Research and Planning, Bureau of Health Professions, Area Resource File, 2000.

OSLDPS—*see* Office for State and Local Domestic Preparedness Support.

Parker, H., *Agricultural Bioterrorism: A Federal Strategy to Meet the Threat,* McNair Paper 65, Washington, D.C.: Institute for National Strategic Studies, National Defense University, March 2002.

Riley, K. J., and B. Hoffman, *Domestic Terrorism: A National Assessment of State and Local Preparedness,* Santa Monica, Calif.: RAND Corporation, MR-505-NIJ, 1995.

Rubin, C. B., W. R. Cumming, I. Renda-Tanali, and T. Birkland, "Major Terrorism Events and Their U.S. Outcomes (1988–2001)," Natural Hazards Research and Applications Information Center, Institute of Behavioral Science, University of Colorado, Boulder, Colo., Natural Hazards Research Working Paper No. 107, March 2003.

Taylor, M. J., R. C. Epper, and T. K. Tolman, "Wireless Communications and Interoperability among State and Local Law Enforcement Agencies," *National Institute of Justice Research in Brief*, Washington, D.C.: U.S. Department of Justice, Office of Justice Programs, National Institute of Justice, January 1998.

U.S. Department of Health and Human Services, "Federal Funds for Public Health Infrastructure Begins to Flow to States," *HHS News*, January 25, 2002, http://www.hhs.gov/news/press/2002pres/20020225a.html.

U.S. Department of Homeland Security, Office of the Inspector General, "An Audit of Distributing and Spending 'First-Responder' Grant Funds," Report No. OIG-04-15, March 2004.

U.S. Department of Homeland Security, Office of the Press Secretary, "Department of Homeland Security Announces Opening of Grant Application Process for Firefighter Assistance Grants," Washington, D.C.: March 10, 2003.

———, "Homeland Security First to Define Interoperability Requirements for Nation's First Responder Community," Washington, D.C., April 26, 2004.

———, "Department of Homeland Security Funding for States and Cities," May 21, 2003.

———, "Secretary of Homeland Security Tom Ridge Visited the National Emergency Training Center," Washington, D.C., June 26, 2003. Online at http://www.dhs.gov/dhspublic/interapp/press_release/press_release_0195.xml (as of February 2, 2004).

U.S. Department of Justice, Counter-Terrorism Training and Resources for Law Enforcement, http://www.counterterrorismtraining.gov/mission/index.html (as of April 30, 2004).

U.S. Department of Justice, Office of the Inspector General, *The Federal Bureau of Investigation's Efforts to Improve the Sharing of Intelligence and Other Information,* Audit Report No. 04-10, December 2003.

U.S. Department of Justice, Office of Justice Programs, The National Criminal Intelligence Sharing Plan, Version 1.0, October 2003.

U.S. General Accounting Office, "Homeland Security: Key Elements of a Risk Management Approach," Statement of Raymond J. Decker, Defense Capabilities and Management, Testimony Before the Subcommittee on National Security, Veterans Affairs, and International Relations, House Committee on Government Reform, Report No. GAO-02-150T, October 12, 2001.

———, "Homeland Security: Efforts to Improve Information Sharing Need to be Strengthened," Report No. GAO-03-760, August 2003.

Waterman, S., "Billions in First-Responder Cash Sits Idle," *Insight on the News*, national issue, February 17, 2004.

White House, Office of the Press Secretary, "Homeland Security Presidential Directive/HSPD-9: Defense of United States Agriculture and Food," Washington, D.C., January 30, 2004.

Wildhorn, S., B. M. Jenkins, and M. M. Lavin, *Intelligence Constraints of the 1970s and Domestic Terrorism*, Vol. 1: *Effects on the Incidence, Investigation, and Prosecution of Terrorist Activity*, Santa Monica, Calif.: RAND Corporation, N-1901-DOJ, December 1982.